Fat Quarterly
Shape
Workshop
for Quilters

Fat Quarterly

Shape Workshop for Quilters

60 Blocks + a Dozen Quilts and Projects

by KATY JONES,
BRIONI GREENBERG,
TACHA BRUECHER
+ JOHN Q. ADAMS

LARK CRAFTS
Asheville

EDITOR
Amanda Carestio

ART DIRECTOR
Megan Kirby

INTERIOR AND
COVER DESIGNER
Pamela Norman

ILLUSTRATOR
Orrin Lundgren

PHOTOGRAPHERS
Patrick Fox,
Steve Mann

PHOTO STYLIST
Lisa Evidon

LARK CRAFTS

An Imprint of Sterling Publishing
387 Park Avenue South
New York, NY 10016

If you have questions or comments about
this book, please visit: larkcrafts.com

Library of Congress Cataloging-in-Publication Data

Fat quarterly shape workshop for quilters : 60 blocks plus a dozen quilts and projects / Katy Jones
... [et al.]. -- 1st ed.

    p. cm.

Includes index.

ISBN 978-1-4547-0282-5

1. Patchwork--Patterns. 2. Quilting--Patterns. 3. Patchwork quilts. 4. Shapes. I. Jones, Katy (Katy
E.) II. Fat quarterly.

TT835.F375 2012

746.46--dc23

                                     2011032110

10 9 8 7 6 5 4 3 2 1

First Edition

Published by Lark Crafts
An Imprint of Sterling Publishing Co., Inc., 387 Park Avenue South, New York, NY 10016

Text © 2012, Katy Jones, Brioni Greenberg, Tacha Bruecher, and John Q. Adams
Photography © 2012, Lark Crafts, an Imprint of Sterling Publishing Co., Inc.
Illustrations © 2012, Lark Crafts, an Imprint of Sterling Publishing Co., Inc.

Distributed in Canada by Sterling Publishing,
c/o Canadian Manda Group, 165 Dufferin Street
Toronto, Ontario, Canada M6K 3H6

Distributed in the United Kingdom by GMC Distribution Services,
Castle Place, 166 High Street, Lewes, East Sussex, England BN7 1XU

Distributed in Australia by Capricorn Link (Australia) Pty Ltd.,
P.O. Box 704, Windsor, NSW 2756 Australia

Manufactured in China

ISBN 13: 978-1-4547-0282-5

For information about custom editions, special sales, premium and corporate purchases, please
contact Sterling Special Sales Department at 800-805-5489 or specialsales@sterlingpub.com.

For information about desk and examination copies available to college and
university professors, requests must be submitted to academic@larkbooks.com. Our complete
policy can be found at www.larkcrafts.com.

contents

introduction

SINCE THIS IS THE INTRODUCTION, we figured we'd start at the beginning: just what (and who) is Fat Quarterly?

It's an e-magazine. Started in the spring of 2010, Fat Quarterly is an e-zine (or electronic magazine) for modern sewists, by modern sewists. The founding members are: Tacha Bruecher, Katy Jones, Brioni Greenberg, and John Q. Adams. We started Fat Quarterly to share project ideas and inspiration within the online quilting community. Each issue is chock full of original patterns and project ideas—compiled in collaboration with fellow members of the creative community—and features new and upcoming fabric lines, articles about developments in the sewing and quilting industry, and interviews with some of the freshest voices in the community. Find more online at **www.fatquarterly.com.**

It's a community. The power of Fat Quarterly is that it's as much about what our readers create as what we do. We strive to create a vibrant community around a shared love of modern sewing and quilting. We love to highlight our readers and their creations—whether from Fat Quarterly patterns or not— via our blog and other platforms, and we've always got an open invitation for pattern and project contributions for our issues.

It's a friendship. Without a doubt, our friendship and the enormous amount of respect we have for one another's talent is the glue that holds our team together. Despite being separated by oceans, having to deal with the communication difficulties caused by time zone differences, and juggling the many demands of our everyday lives, the bond we've created and the generous support of our readers and the quilting industry keeps us—and our creation— going strong.

And now, it's a book!

connect with us online!

www.fatquarterly.com
www.twitter.com/fatquarterly
www.facebook.com/fatquarterly

WELCOME TO THE *Fat Quarterly* SHAPE WORKSHOP FOR QUILTERS!

FAT QUARTERLY SHAPE WORKSHOP FOR QUILTERS is the ultimate guide to understanding and incorporating shapes into your quilt projects. The premise is actually based on a regular column in our online magazine called the Design Challenge, in which a design panel is given a block layout, fabric swatch, or color palette as inspiration and asked to design a quilt block. In this book, we've turned our focus to shapes and how to use them as inspiration in sewing and quilting projects.

The Shape Workshop presents six common quilting shapes used in dynamic and exciting ways: squares and rectangles, triangles, circles, polygons, diamonds, and stars. For each shape, you'll find 10 different quilt blocks from traditional to modern designs (each sized to a finished 12 inches [30.5 cm]) followed by a quilted project and a full-size quilt, perfect for trying a particular shape out on a larger-scale project.

Along your journey you'll learn appliqué, machine piecing, hand piecing, and how to utilize shapes in your projects as well as mastering curved seams with clear instructions, diagrams, templates, and beautiful photographs. Need a quick refresher in quilting basics? We've provided that, too; take a peek at page 130.

Maybe you need inspiration for a quilting bee? Or maybe you want to try something new? This book is an invaluable tool for anyone starting out in quilting as well as those with a desire to push their skills a little further. And it's full of the stuff we love: stunning quilts (of course!), smaller projects (think placemats, pillows, and even a clock!) perfect for gifting or practice, and block patterns to mix and match and customize your own projects. We've also varied the techniques we used so that no matter your skill level—whether beginner or advanced—there's something in this book for you.

welcome

about us

We are a team of four quilters spread across the globe, brought together by our love of the craft and our mutual admiration of one another's work. We met each other through virtual quilting and sewing communities via blogs, swaps, and online photo sharing sites. We work together to produce our quarterly e-zine... and this book. (P.S. We wrote these bios for each other.)

Tacha Bruecher

Katy Jones

Brioni Greenberg

John Q. Adams

Currently living in Berlin, Germany, **Tacha Bruecher** is an amazingly talented sewist whose skills stretch far beyond quilting. Although she enjoys handmade crafts from jewelry making and screen-printing to knitting and stamp carving, she considers quilting her true love and excels at intricate piecing and hand sewing. She blogs at Hanies (http://haniesquilts.blogspot.com).

Katy Jones is a colorful, energetic, and tattooed quilter living in the U.K. Her blog, I'm a Ginger Monkey (http://imagingermonkey.blogspot.com), quickly captured the attention of crafters around the world not only because of Katy's talent, but because of her infectious personality and unique style. Katy appreciates the history of the art of quilting and loves to blend the old with the new to create her signature style.

Brioni Greenberg is also a U.K.-based crafter who continuously amazes the many followers of her blog, FlossyBlossy (http://flossyblossy.blogspot.com), with her impeccable taste, her ability to combine colors and fabrics in new and interesting ways, and her fearless approach to tackling the most advanced sewing and quilting techniques. Swappers around the world covet the beautiful things that Brioni so generously makes for others, which always seem to be at once precious and sophisticated.

John Q. Adams is a hugely talented and well-respected quilter from the United States. His blog, Quilt Dad (http://www.quiltdad.com), has commanded a large and loyal following thanks to his charming personality and fresh twists on modern quilting. John has been published in various quilting books and has had works displayed in many designers' booths at International Quilt Market.

squares & rectangles

WE CAN'T REALLY TALK ABOUT shapes in quilting without starting with our reliable, go-to guys: the square and the rectangle. Squares and rectangles— basically, any shape with four sides and containing four 90˚ angles—are the best place for a beginning quilter to start. Squares and rectangles are easy to cut and easier to match points than triangles or curved piecing. And stitching basic squares and rectangles together is the perfect way to prac- tice making ¼-inch (6 mm) seams and matching corners.

But if you think that sewing with squares and rectangles is beginners- only territory, think again. In fact, these simple shapes can be combined in seemingly infinite ways to form quilt patterns that are new and innovative, traditional or contemporary, exact or "wonky." Beginning and advanced quilt- ers alike continue to create amazing quilts with tried-and-true block patterns such as log cabin, courthouse steps, four-patch, and nine-patch blocks. All are composed of the most basic square and rectangle shapes.

Simple. Approachable, timeless, versatile. What can you create with squares and rectangles?

book of stamps

by KATY JONES

CUTTING

1 From assorted print fabrics of dark and light colors, cut 24 squares measuring 1½ inches (3.8 cm).

2 From white solid fabric, cut the following strips for the outer border:
- ☐ 2 strips measuring 3½ x 8½ inches (8.9 x 21.6 cm)
- ☐ 2 strips measuring 2½ x 12½ inches (6.4 x 31.8 cm)

3 From red solid fabric, cut the following strips for the inner border:
- ☐ 2 strips measuring 1½ x 4½ inches (3.8 x 11.4 cm)
- ☐ 2 strips measuring 1½ x 6½ inches (3.8 x 16.5 cm)

ASSEMBLY

4 Stitch the 1½-inch (3.8 cm) squares into four rows of six squares, alternating dark and light squares **(FIGURE 1)**. Press seams to the dark fabric.

5 Stitch the two longer red border strips to the top and bottom of the block. Press seams towards the border. Stitch the remaining red inner border strips to the sides of the block.

6 Stitch the two shorter white border strips to the top and bottom of the block. Press seams towards the inner border. Stitch the remaining white border strips to the sides of the block.

FIGURE 1

> I have been wanting to make a postage stamp quilt for the longest time, but the thought of making a whole quilt using just 1-inch [2.5 cm] squares is daunting. This block is a far easier way to scratch that postage stamp itch!
>
> — Katy

a dime a dozen

by TACHA BRUECHER

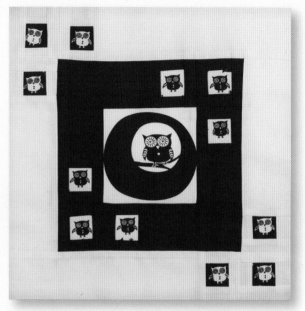

CUTTING

1 From print fabric, cut one 4½-inch (11.4 cm) square for the center.

2 Fussy-cut the small featured squares as follows:
- From red-on-white print: 6 squares measuring 1½ inches (3.8 cm)
- From white-on-red print: 6 squares measuring 1½ inches (3.8 cm)

3 From red solid fabric, cut the following:
- 2 strips measuring 2½ x 3 inches (6.4 x 7.6 cm)
- 2 strips measuring 2½ x 5 inches (6.4 x 12.7 cm)
- 12 strips measuring 1 x 1½ inches (2.5 x 3.8 cm)
- 8 strips measuring 1 x 2½ inches (2.5 x 6.4 cm)

4 From white solid fabric, cut the following:
- 2 strips measuring 2½ x 9 inches (2.5 x 22.9 cm)
- 2 strips measuring 2½ x 7 inches (2.5 x 17.8 cm)
- 12 strips measuring 1 x 1½ inches (2.5 x 3.8 cm)
- 8 strips measuring 1 x 2½ inches (2.5 x 6.4 cm)

ASSEMBLY

5 Stitch the first red blocks as follows **(FIGURE 2)**. Check each time that the image in the print block is oriented right side up.
- **Block A:** Select one red-on-white print square, and two short and two long red 1½-inch (3.8 cm) strips. Stitch the two short strips to the sides of the square and press. Then stitch the long strips to the top and bottom edges.
- **Block B:** Stitch two short red 1½-inch (3.8 cm) strips to the top and bottom of a red-on-white print block. Press. Stitch a long red 1½-inch (3.8 cm) strip to the left and a 2½ x 7-inch (6.4 x 13.25 cm) red strip to the right.
- **Block C:** Repeat the instructions for block B, but with the side pieces reversed to make a mirror image of B.

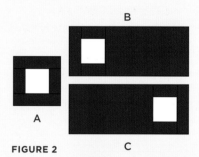

FIGURE 2

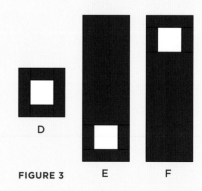

FIGURE 3

6 Stitch the remaining red blocks as follows **(FIGURE 3)**.
- □ **Block D:** Stitch as for block A, but with the short red strips on the top and bottom, and the long strips on the sides.
- □ **Block E:** Stitch two short red 1½-inch (3.8cm) strips to the sides of a red-and-white print block. Press. Stitch a long red 1½-inch (3.8 cm) strip to the bottom and a 2½ x 9-inch (6.4 x 22.9 cm) red strip to the top.
- □ **Block F:** Repeat the instructions for block E, but with the top and bottom pieces reversed to make a mirror image of E.

7 Stitch the white blocks together in the same way as the red blocks **(FIGURES 4 AND 5)**.

8 Assemble the red strips and the center square as shown **(FIGURE 6)**.
- □ Stitch the A block to the top of the F block.
- □ Stitch the B block to the top of the center square and the C block to the bottom.
- □ Stitch the D block to the bottom of the E block.
- □ Stitch the columns together, left to right.

9 Add the white strips to the outside edges as shown **(FIGURE 6)**.

> I designed this block to be the perfect showcase for little motifs. Just reverse each alternate block, and you can make a whole quilt with little motifs zigzagging across it. — Tacha

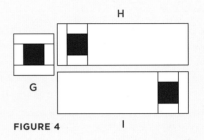

FIGURE 4

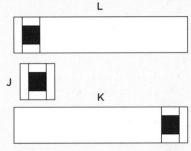

FIGURE 5

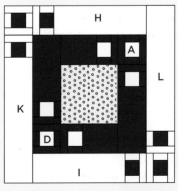

FIGURE 6

deck of cards

by JOHN Q. ADAMS

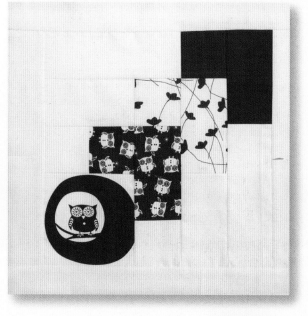

CUTTING

1 From print fabric, fussy-cut one square measuring 4½ inches (11.4 cm). In the example, the owl is on the lower left.

2 From each of three print fabrics, cut the following:
- 1 square measuring 2½ inches (6.4 cm)
- 1 rectangle measuring 2½ x 4½ inches (6.4 x 11.4 cm)

3 From white solid fabric, cut:
- 2 squares measuring 2½ inches (6.4 cm)
- 2 rectangles measuring 2½ x 4½ inches (6.4 x 11.4 cm)
- 2 rectangles measuring 2½ x 6½ inches (6.4 x 16.5 cm)
- 2 strips measuring 1½ x 10½ inches (3.8 x 26.7 cm)
- 2 strips measuring 1½ x 12½ inches (3.8 x 31.8 cm)

ASSEMBLY

4 To make the first block **(FIGURE 7)**:
- Stitch a print square to white solid square, and press seams to the print side.
- Stitch a rectangle of the same print to the remaining white solid square and press.
- Stitch the pieced strips to the 4½-inch (11.4 cm) square as shown.

5 Add to the block as follows **(FIGURE 8)**:
- Stitch another print square to a 2½ x 4½-inch (6.4 x 11.4 cm) white solid rectangle.
- Stitch a rectangle of the same print to the remaining 2½ x 4½-inch (6.4 x 11.4 cm) white solid rectangle.
- Stitch these two strips to the first print block as shown.
- Repeat with the remaining print fabrics and the 2½ x 6½-inch (6.4 x 16.5 cm) white solid rectangles.

6 Add the white strips as a border:
- Stitch the 1½ x 10½ inches (3.8 x 26.7 cm) strips to the sides of the block.
- Stitch the 1½ x 12½inches (3.8 x 31.8 cm) strips to the top and bottom.

FIGURE 7

FIGURE 8

Instead of limiting myself to two dimensions, I decided to try to introduce more depth into this block design. Clever piecing gives the effect of stacked or overlapping squares.
— John

windowpane

by BRIONI GREENBERG

CUTTING

1 From white background fabric, cut:
- ☐ 2 strips measuring 1½ x 4½ inches (3.8 x 11.4 cm)
- ☐ 2 strips measuring 1½ x 6½ inches (3.8 x 16.5 cm)
- ☐ 2 strips measuring 1½ x 10½ inches (3.8 x 26.7 cm)
- ☐ 2 strips measuring 1½ x 12½ inches (3.8 x 31.8 cm)

2 From coordinating print fabrics, cut:
- ☐ 1 fussy-cut square for the center measuring 4½ inches (11.4 cm)
- ☐ 12 squares measuring 2½ inches (6.4 cm)

3 From red solid fabric, cut four squares measuring 2½ inches (6.4 cm).

ASSEMBLY

4 Stitch the center block as follows:
- ☐ Stitch the two 4½-inch (11.4cm) white background strips to the sides of the center square.
- ☐ Stitch the two 6½-inch (16.5 cm) white background strips to the top and bottom.

5 Assemble the 2½-inch (6.4 cm) print squares:
- ☐ Stitch four strips with three coordinating prints. To match the example, select one of the fabrics to be the center of each strip.
- ☐ To two of those strips, stitch solid red squares on both ends.

6 Stitch the shorter three-square strips to the sides of the center block. Stitch the longer five-square strips to the top and bottom.

7 To finish the block, stitch the shorter remaining white strips to the sides of the block, then stitch the longer remaining white strips to the top and bottom.

crooked frames

by KATY JONES

CUTTING

note: *The "rings" of color around the center block are numbered 1 through 5, starting with the innermost red ring around the center square.*

1 From print fabric, cut the following.
- ☐ 1 fussy-cut square for the center, measuring 2 inches (5.1 cm)
- ☐ 1 strip for ring 2 measuring 1½ x 4 inches (3.8 x 10.2 cm)
- ☐ 2 strips for ring 2 measuring 1½ x 5 inches (3.8 x 12.7cm)
- ☐ 1 strip for ring 2 measuring 1½ x 6 inches (3.8 x 15.2 cm)
- ☐ 1 strip for ring 4 measuring 1½ x 8 inches (3.8 x 20.3 cm)
- ☐ 2 strips for ring 4 measuring 1½ x 9 inches (3.8x 22.9 cm)
- ☐ 1 strip for ring 4 measuring 1½ x 10 inches (3.8 x 25.4 cm)

2 From red solid fabric, cut:
- ☐ 1 strip for ring 1 measuring 1½ x 2 inches (3.8 x 5.1 cm)
- ☐ 2 strips for ring 1 measuring 1½ x 3 inches (3.8 x 7.6 cm)
- ☐ 1 strip for ring 1 measuring 1½ x 4 inches (3.8 x 10.2 cm)
- ☐ 1 strip for ring 3 measuring 1½ x 6 inches (3.8 x 15.2cm)
- ☐ 2 strips for ring 3 measuring 1½ x 7 inches (3.8 x 17.8 cm)
- ☐ 1 strip for ring 3 measuring 1½ x 8 inches (3.8 x 20.3 cm)
- ☐ 1 strip for ring 5 measuring 3 x 10 inches (7.6 x 25.4 cm)
- ☐ 2 strips for ring 5 measuring 3 x 13½ inches (7.6 x 34.3 cm)
- ☐ 1 strip for ring 5 measuring 3 x 16½ inches (7.6 x 41.9 cm)

ASSEMBLY

3 Construct the block in five rings as if sewing a log cabin. Starting with the shortest strip in each ring, stitch the strips in a clockwise direction around the center square **(FIGURE 9)**.

4 To create the crooked effect, lay a 12½-inch (31.8 cm) square ruler on top of the pieced block, and angle it to one side. Trim the block to a 12½-inch (31.8 cm) square **(FIGURE 10)**.

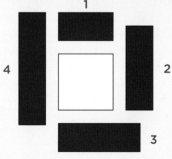

FIGURE 9

FIGURE 10

cross block

by KATY JONES

CUTTING

1 From white solid fabric, cut:
- ☐ 4 squares measuring 4½ inches (11.4 cm)
- ☐ 4 rectangles measuring 2½ x 4½ inches (6.4 x 11.4 cm)

2 From red print fabric, cut:
- ☐ 1 square measuring 4½ inches (11.4 cm)
- ☐ 4 rectangles measuring 2½ x 4½ inches
  (6.4 cm x 11.4 cm)

- -

ASSEMBLY

3 Stitch a red rectangle to a white rectangle to form a square. Press seams to the dark side. Repeat with all rectangles to form a total of four pieced squares.

4 Stitch the block together in rows, referring to the block diagram **(FIGURE 13)**.

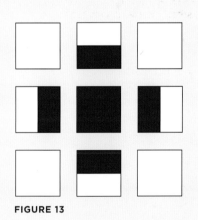

FIGURE 13

owl in the corner

by KATY JONES

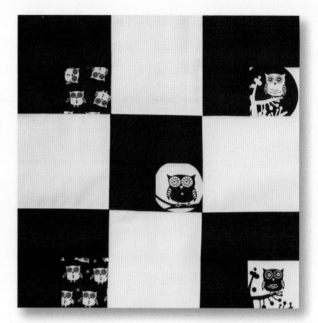

CUTTING

1 From white solid fabric, cut four squares measuring 4½ inches (11.4 cm).

2 From red solid fabric, cut:
- 5 rectangles measuring 2½ x 4½ inches (6.4 x 11.4 cm)
- 5 squares measuring 2½ inches (6.4 cm)

3 From print fabric, fussy-cut five squares measuring 2½ inches (6.4 cm).

- -

ASSEMBLY

4 Stitch a red 2½-inch (6.4 cm) square to the left of each fussy-cut square. Press seams to the red fabric.

5 Stitch a red rectangle to the top of each pieced fussy-cut strip. Press seams toward the rectangle.

6 Arrange the squares as shown **(FIGURE 14)** and stitch together in rows. Ensure that the fussy cut pieces are in the bottom right-hand corner of each square.

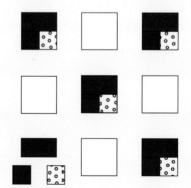

FIGURE 14

gift boxes
by BRIONI GREENBERG

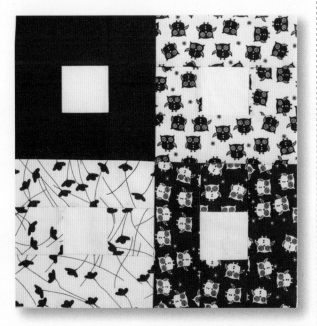

CUTTING

1 From white solid fabric, cut four squares measuring 2½ inches (6.4 cm).

2 From each of four print fabrics, cut the following:
- ☐ 2 squares measuring 2½ inches (6.4 cm)
- ☐ 2 strips measuring 2½ x 6½ inches (6.4 cm x 16.5 cm)

- -

ASSEMBLY

3 To make each block:
- ☐ Select two matching print squares and stitch them to both sides of a white square. Press the seams away from the white square.
- ☐ Stitch the two matching print rectangles to the top and bottom of the pieced strip.
- ☐ Make a total of four blocks.

4 Lay the four blocks together to form one large block. In the example, the blocks are turned so that each pieced row abuts a rectangle. Stitch the blocks together, pressing seams as you go.

cub crawl baby quilt

by John Q. Adams ■ finished size: 48 x 56 inches (121.9 x 142.2 cm)
■ machine quilted by Angela Walters

Cub Crawl combines square-in-square blocks with long rectangles to create a design perfect for highlighting both fussy-cut squares as well as large prints. Although it's a beginner-friendly pattern, the versatility of the design for different color and pattern combinations can appeal to all skill levels.

materials

- ☐ ½ yard (.5 m) cuts of seven assorted prints
- ☐ 4 fat quarters of coordinating solid or near-solid fabrics
- ☐ 3½ yards (3.2 m) of backing fabric
- ☐ 1 piece of batting, 56 x 64 inches (142.2 x 162.6 cm)
- ☐ ½ yard (.5 m) of binding fabric

cutting

1 From the assorted prints, cut a total of:
- ☐ 14 squares measuring 4½ inches (11.4 cm)
- ☐ 12 rectangles measuring 4½ x 8½ inches (11.4 cm x 21.6 cm)
- ☐ 22 rectangles measuring 4½ x 16½ inches (11.4 cm x 41.9 cm)

note: *Distribute the squares and rectangles between your prints to add variety.*

2 From each fat quarter, cut the following **(FIGURE 15)**:
- ☐ 8 rectangles measuring 2½ x 4½ inches (6.4 cm x 11.4 cm)
- ☐ 8 rectangles measuring 2½ x 8½ inches (6.4 cm x 21.6 cm)

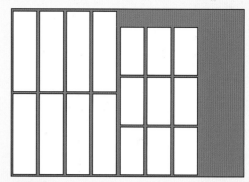

FIGURE 15

assembly

3 To make each frame block **(FIGURE 16)**:
- ☐ Stitch a 2½ x 4½-inch (6.4x 11.4cm) solid strip to the top and bottom of a 4½-inch (11.4 cm) print square.
- ☐ Stitch a 2½ x 8½-inch (6.4 x 21.6 cm) solid strip to the left and right sides of the block.
- ☐ Repeat to make 16 framed blocks, mixing up your prints and solids as desired.

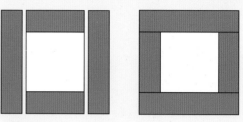

FIGURE 16

4 Pair up the 4½ x 8½-inch (11.4 x 21.6 cm) print rectangles. Stitch each pair together along the long edge to make 6 blocks measuring 8½ inches (21.6 cm) square.

note: *Take note of directional fabrics, and keep them facing right side up.*

5 Pair up the 4½ x 16½-inch (11.4 x 41.9cm) print rectangles. Stitch each pair together along a long edge to make 11 blocks measuring 8½ x 16½ inches (21.6 x 41.9 cm).

6 Assemble the quilt tops in rows according to the diagram **(FIGURE 17)**.

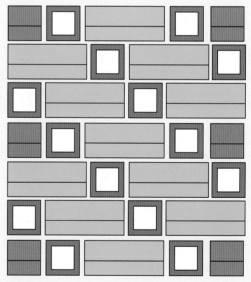

FIGURE 17

7 Refer to pages 135-137 for tips on basting, quilting, and binding your quilt.

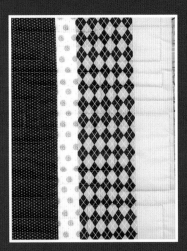

his hope chest

by Katy Jones ■ finished size: 68 x 90 inches (172.7 x 228.6 cm)
■ machine quilted by Christine Marriage using "Square Dance"
by Karen Thompson

The tradition of collecting treasured items in a hope chest might be a little outdated these days, but the principle is a lovely one for both girls and boys. This quilt can be made for a little boy (or in more feminine colors for a little girl) and features a double-sided design to last through the years.

materials

- ☐ 5 fat quarters of print fabric for block A
- ☐ 4 fat quarters of print fabric for block B
- ☐ ⅝ yard (.6 m) of charcoal solid fabric
- ☐ ⅞ yard (.8 m) of pale blue solid fabric (front side)
- ☐ 2¾ yard (2.5 m) of white solid fabric (front side)
- ☐ 1 yard (.9 m) of brown solid fabric (back side)
- ☐ 4½ yards (4 m) of cream solid fabric (back side)
- ☐ 1 piece of batting, 77 x 100 inches (195.6 x 254 cm)
- ☐ ¾ yard (.7m) of fabric for binding (or use leftovers from the fat quarters)

cutting

1 From each of the fat quarters for block A, cut the following strips **(FIGURE 18)**, and set aside the leftover fabric for binding. To save time, cut the 18-inch (45.7 cm) side to 15½ inches (39.4 cm) first, then cut the widths:

☐ 1 strip measuring 5½ x 15½ inches (14 x 39.4 cm)

☐ 1 strip measuring 4½ x 15½ inches (11.4 x 39.4 cm)

☐ 1 strip measuring 3½ x 15½ inches (8.9 x 39.4 cm)

☐ 1 strip measuring 2½ x 15½ inches (6.4 x 39.4 cm)

☐ 1 strip measuring 1½ x 15½ inches (3.8x 39.4 cm)

2 From each of the fat quarters for block B, cut the following strips **(FIGURE 19)**, and set aside the leftover fabric for binding. Once again, cut the 15½-inch (39.4 cm) length first.

☐ 1 strip measuring 5½ x 15½ inches (14 x 39.4cm)

☐ 1 strip measuring 4½ x 15½ inches (11.4 x 39.4cm)

☐ 1 strip measuring 3½ x 15½ inches (8.9 x 39.4 cm)

☐ 1 strip measuring 2½ x 15½ inches (6.4 x 39.4 cm)

3 From the charcoal solid fabric, cut the following:

☐ 5 strips measuring 2½ inches (6.4 cm) x the width of the fabric, for the front of the quilt

☐ 12 strips measuring 1½ x 15½ inches (3.8 x 39.4 cm), for block B

4 From the blue solid fabric, cut five strips measuring 5½ inches (14 cm) x the width of fabric.

5 From the white solid fabric, cut two pieces measuring 20 x 90 inches (50.8 x 228.6cm).

6 From the brown solid fabric, cut out the following pieces and set aside the leftover fabric for binding:

☐ 6 strips measuring 2½ x 15½ inches (6.4x 39.4 cm)

☐ 6 strips measuring 2½ x 19½ inches (6.4 x 49.5 cm)

☐ 4 strips measuring 5½ x 19½ inches (14 x 49.5 cm)

7 From the cream solid fabric, cut two strips measuring 77 inches (195.6 cm) x the width of the fabric.

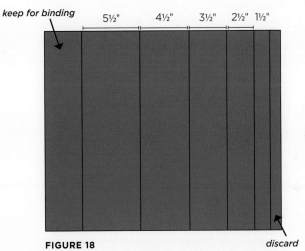

keep for binding   5½"   4½"   3½"   2½" 1½"

FIGURE 18   discard

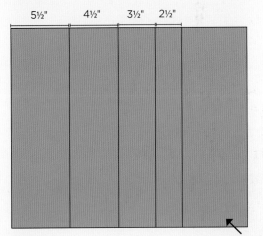

5½"   4½"   3½"   2½"

FIGURE 19   keep for binding

assembly

8 To make each block A, select five strips from different block A fabrics, one of each width size, and lay them side by side. Stitch them together, press, and trim as needed to form a block measuring 15½ inches (39.4 cm) square **(FIGURE 20)**. Make a total of five blocks.

9 To make each block B, select four strips from different block B fabrics, one of each width size. Lay them side by side with a 15½-inch (39.4cm) charcoal strip between each print. Stitch the strips together, press, and trim as needed to form a block measuring 15½ inches (39.4cm) square **(FIGURE 21)**. Make a total of four blocks.

10 To assemble the back of the quilt **(FIGURE 22)**:

☐ Form the center strip by arranging 6 blocks in a row from top to bottom: A, B, A, B, A, B. Turn all A blocks so the strips run vertically, and turn the B blocks with strips running horizontally. Stitch the blocks together and press.

☐ Stitch the 2½-inch (6.4 cm) charcoal strips together end-to-end to make one long strip. Cut the strip into two pieces each measuring 90 inches (228.6 cm) in length. Stitch a charcoal strip to each side of the pieced center strip. Press seams towards the charcoal strip.

☐ Stitch the blue strips end-to-end in the same way to make one length, then cut into two pieces, each 90 inches (228.6 cm) long. Stitch a blue strip to each side of the charcoal strips and press seams towards the blue strips.

☐ Stitch a white section to each of the blue strips and press seams towards the blue strips.

☐ At this point, your finished quilt top should measure approximately 68 x 90 inches (172.7 x 228.6 cm).

11 To assemble the front of the quilt **(FIGURE 23)**:

☐ Frame each remaining three A and B blocks with brown strips by stitching the 2½ x 15½-inch (6.4 x 39.4 cm) strips to the sides and stitching the 2½ x 19½-inch (6.4 x 49.5 cm) strips to the top and bottom. Press seams towards the brown fabric.

☐ Form the center strip by arranging the blocks A, B, A, with a 5½ x 19½-inch (14 x 49.5 cm) brown block between each block and on the ends.

☐ Stitch the row together and press seams to one side. The finished strip should measure 77 inches (195.6 cm).

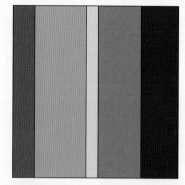

FIGURE 20

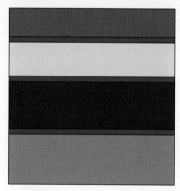

FIGURE 21

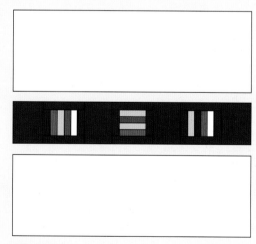

FIGURE 22

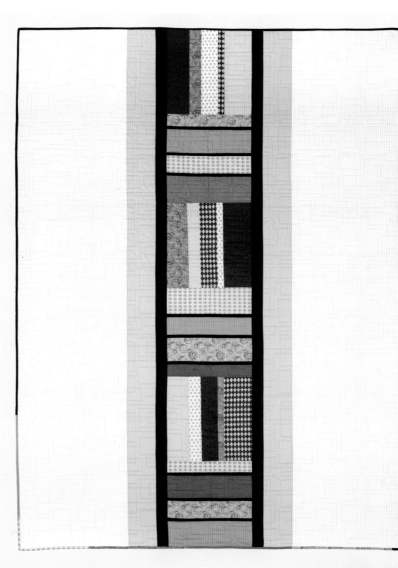

- ☐ Stitch a cream strip to either side of the center strip and press seams to the darker fabric.
- ☐ Your finished quilt back should measure approximately 77 x 100 inches (195.6 x 254 cm), with extra to allow for the long arm quilting process.

12 Refer to pages 135-137 for tips on basting, quilting, and binding your quilt. To achieve the scrappy look of the binding in the example, cut strips 2½ inches (6.4 cm) wide from your leftover fabrics and stitch them end-to-end to make one long strip. You will need 330 inches (838.2 cm) of binding for this quilt. For a more uniform look, cut the binding from one fabric.

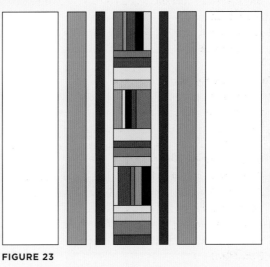

FIGURE 23

circles

WHAT TWO WORDS STRIKE FEAR into the heart of many quilters, even the most seasoned among them? (No, it's not "empty stash"!) If you guessed "curved piecing," then you're probably right. When cutting and sewing curved edges, most quilters agree on three basic rules: pin, pin, and pin some more. And really, there isn't much more to it than that. If you take the time to carefully pin your pieces together and sew them slowly and deliberately, easing the pieces through your machine, it won't take much prac-tice before you are successful. Trust us on this one.

But if curved piecing is not your thing, there are alternative ways to incorporate circles into your quilting projects. In fact, adding circles to your quilt design is the perfect way to use and develop various appliqué techniques in your sewing repertoire. Whether it's raw-edge, needle-turn, or reverse appliqué, consider approaching your quilt design armed with these skills.

So what are you waiting for? The time to be afraid of curved piecing is over. No matter your skill (or confidence) level, you're sure to find a safe place to begin your journey with circles.

There's no need to be afraid of circles in patchwork: curves are cool!

circle nine-patch

by BRIONI GREENBERG

CUTTING

note: *In addition to fabric, you will also need template plastic and fusible web.*

1 From scraps of printed fabric, cut the following:
- ☐ 9 squares measuring 4½ inches (11.4cm) for the background
- ☐ 9 squares measuring 3 inches (7.6 cm) for cutting circles

- -

ASSEMBLY

2 Stitch together the 4½-inch (11.4 cm) background squares into three rows of three squares. Stitch the rows together to form a nine-patch block.

3 Draw a 3-inch (7.6 cm) circle onto template plastic and cut it out. Trace around the template on the paper backing of the fusible web to make nine circles. Roughly cut out the circles.

4 Press fusible web pieces onto the 3-inch (7.6 cm) fabric squares, following the manufacturer's directions. Cut out the circles along the drawn lines.

5 Peel off the paper backing and center a circle in each nine-patch square, allowing for the ¼-inch (6 mm) seam on the outer edge of the block. Once you are happy with the placement, press the circles to adhere them to the background.

6 Stitch around the edge of the circles to permanently attach them to the background.

infinite loop

by JOHN Q. ADAMS

CUTTING

1 From print fabric, cut two squares measuring 6½ inches (16.5 cm) for the plain squares.

2 From focus print fabric, cut three squares measuring 8½ inches (21.6 cm) for the curved piecing.

- -

ASSEMBLY

3 Stack the three focus print squares on top of each other, right sides up, aligning the corners of the squares. Cut them as follows **(FIGURE 1)**:

□ With a rotary cutter, make a freehand curved cut in one corner of the stack, approximately one-third of the way in from the bottom left corner to approximately one-third of the way up from the bottom left corner. Leave the fabrics in place to make your second cut.

□ Make another freehand curved cut approximately 2 to 3 inches (5.1 to 7.6 cm) from where your first cut started and ended.

4 Rearrange the pieces to form an inner, middle, and outer section from the three different prints.

□ Pin and stitch the smallest inner section to the middle section along the curved edge.

□ Pin and stitch this piece to the largest outer section along the curved edge.

□ Press the block and trim to a 6½-inch (16.5 cm) square.

5 Repeat step 4 with another grouping of inner, middle, and outer pieces.

note: *You will have three pieces leftover.*

6 Stitch together the four 6½-inch (16.5 cm) quadrants using the block photo as a guide for placement.

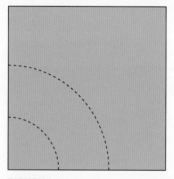

FIGURE 1

orange soda redux

by KATY JONES

CUTTING

note: *In addition to fabrics, you will also need fusible web and some template plastic.*

1 From fabric scraps, cut 16 squares measuring 3½ inches (8.9 cm).

2 From contrasting fabric (for the petals), cut one square measuring 9 inches (22.9 cm).

3 Enlarge the petal template on page 138. Trace it onto template plastic and cut it out.

4 Adhere the fusible web to the wrong side of the 9-inch (22.9 cm) square of contrasting fabric, following the manufacturer's instructions. Trace, and cut out 16 petal shapes.

- -

ASSEMBLY

5 To make the block **(FIGURE 2)**:
- ☐ Stitch the 3½-inch (8.9 cm) squares together in four rows of four squares each.
- ☐ Peel the paper off each petal shape as you press them diagonally across the block, centered on top of the seams as shown.
- ☐ Use matching thread to stitch the appliqués in place.

FIGURE 2

modern wheel

by TACHA BRUECHER

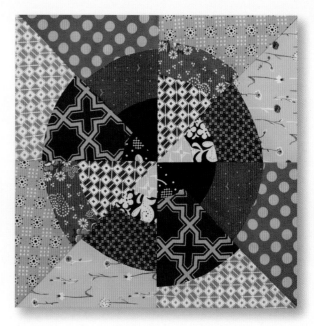

CUTTING

1 From green prints, cut the following:
- ☐ 3 squares measuring 8 inches (20.3cm)
- ☐ 1 square measuring 8½ inches (21.6 cm)
   (for the four-ring square)

2 From assorted fabrics, cut out the following pieces:
- ☐ plum prints, 4 squares measuring 6 inches (15.2 cm)
- ☐ brown prints, 4 squares measuring 6 inches (15.2 cm)
- ☐ yellow print, 1 square measuring 6 inches (15.2 cm)

3 Use a compass or trace around lids or dishes to cut nine paper circles varying in size from 5 to 12 inches (12.7 to 30.5 cm) across. Fold the circles into quarters, and leave folded to make the templates for your wheel.

FIGURE 3

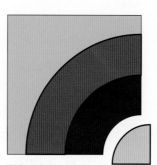

FIGURE 4

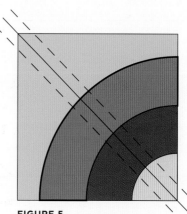

FIGURE 5

ASSEMBLY

4 To make a quarter-circle unit:

☐ Place the largest quarter-circle on the back of a 6-inch (15.2 cm) plum square, matching up the point with a corner. Trace the shape and cut it out. Trace the same quarter-circle in the corner of an 8-inch (20.3 cm) green square. Cut it out. Discard the green quarter-circle and keep what's left in the corner.

☐ Stitch the two cut shapes together. Find the center point of the curved edges on each piece and match them up, right sides facing. Carefully pin the fabrics together, easing the fabric as you go. Stitch, open the fabrics, and press.

☐ Use the next-largest quarter-circle to trace and cut from a brown fabric square. Cut the same shape from the pieced quarter-circle fabric and discard the quarter-circle. Stitch together as shown **(FIGURE 3)**.

5 Make three more quarter-circle blocks in the same way, using different-sized quarter circles and the remaining 8- and 8½-inch (20.3 and 21.6 cm) squares.

6 Repeat the process again with the 8½-inch (20.3 cm) square, this time tracing the smallest quarter-circle onto yellow fabric. Complete the stitching as shown **(FIGURE 4)**. Trim all the squares to 7 inches (17.8 cm).

7 Once you've made four quarter-circle squares, arrange them in pairs. Draw a line down the diagonal on the backside of one square. With each pair together, right sides facing, stitch ¼ inch (6 mm) away from the drawn line on both sides **(FIGURE 5)**. Cut along the diagonal line, open, and press. Trim each square to 6½ inches (16.5 cm).

8 Arrange the four squares into a block, with matched halves on opposite corners, and stitch them together to make the wheel **(FIGURE 6)**.

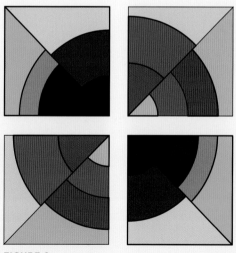

FIGURE 6

quarter twist

by TACHA BRUECHER

CUTTING

note: *In addition to fabrics, you will also need template plastic.*

1 From assorted coordinating fabrics, cut out the following pieces:

- ☐ plum prints, four squares measuring 4 inches (10.2 cm)
- ☐ coordinating yellow prints, four squares measuring 2 inches (5.1 cm)
- ☐ green prints, eight rectangles measuring 4 x 5 inches (10.2 x 12.7 cm)
- ☐ brown prints, four squares measuring 5 inches (12.7 cm)

ASSEMBLY

2 Enlarge the templates (A, B, C, D, and E) on page 138. Trace them onto template plastic and cut them out.

3 Trace the following template shapes on the wrong side of the following fabrics and cut them out:

- ☐ Template A on the four plum print squares.
- ☐ Template B on the four yellow print squares.

4 Stitch each yellow B piece to a plum A piece **(FIGURE 7)**.

FIGURE 7

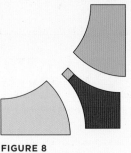

FIGURE 8

5 Trace template C on the wrong side of four green fabric squares and cut them out. Trace template D on the remaining four green squares and cut them out. Stitch a C piece and a D piece to either side of the plum/yellow piece **(FIGURE 8)**. Repeat for the remaining plum/yellow pieces.

6 Trace template E on the wrong side of the four brown squares and cut them out. As in the last step, fold and crease the center of each curved edge. Pin the center of an E shape to the center of the yellow square in each pieced block **(FIGURE 9)**. Ease and pin the edges together, then stitch. Press the finished block; it will measure 6½ inches (16.5 cm) square.

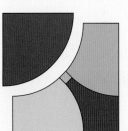

FIGURE 9

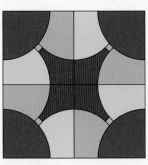

FIGURE 10

7 Stitch the blocks together in rows, then stitch the two rows together, matching the center seams **(FIGURE 10)**.

scrappy circle

by BRIONI GREENBERG

CUTTING

note: *In addition to fabrics, you will also need template plastic.*

1 From background fabric, cut four squares measuring 6½ inches (16.5 cm).

2 From fabric scraps, cut 32 pieces that measure 2 x 2½ inches (5.1 x 6.4 cm).

- -

ASSEMBLY

3 Enlarge the templates on page 139.
  □ Trace templates A and B onto template plastic and cut them out. Label each of the templates on the right side.
  □ Make four copies of template C on printer paper.

4 Trace around templates A and B on the wrong side of each background fabric square and cut out the shapes.

5 With the template C copies, use the foundation paper piecing method (page 134) to sew scrappy fabric arcs:
  □ Start by positioning one of the fabric scraps at the center of the paper template. Then stitch fabrics scraps to both sides, sewing through both the paper and the fabric.
  □ Continue until the template is completely covered.
  □ Cut along the template outline and carefully remove the paper.
  □ Repeat to make four arcs.

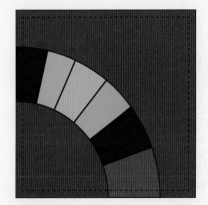

FIGURE 11

6 To complete a block **(FIGURE 11)**:
  □ Stitch the outside edge of each arc to a template A piece. Press the seam in the direction of the pieced arc.
  □ Stitch the inside edge of each arc to a template B piece. Press the seam in the direction of the pieced arc.

7 Stitch the four quadrants together.

wonky bulls-eye
by KATY JONES

CUTTING

1 From assorted fabrics, cut the following:
- ☐ Approximately 20 strips that are at least 3 x 8 inches (7.6 x 20.3 cm)
- ☐ 4 scraps measuring 2½ inches (6.4 cm) square

ASSEMBLY

2 To make one of the quarter-blocks **(FIGURE 12)**:
- ☐ Select one of the squares and cut a gentle convex (outwards) curve from corner to opposite corner.
- ☐ Select a strip that is about twice the length of the curved piece. Cut a strip freehand with a concave (inward) curve to match the convex curve of the first piece.
- ☐ Match the center point of each curve and stitch the two pieces with right sides together.
- ☐ Press the seam towards the second piece.
- ☐ Continue to cut strips of varying widths and stitching them together until you have a block slightly larger than 7 inches (17.8 cm) square.

3 Press the block well, using steam if necessary to make it lie flat. Square up the block to 6½ inches (16.5 cm) **(FIGURE 13)**.

4 Repeat steps 2 and 3 to make a total of four blocks. Arrange them to form a rough bulls-eye. Stitch them together, and trim to 12½ inches (31.8 cm).

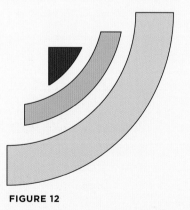

FIGURE 12

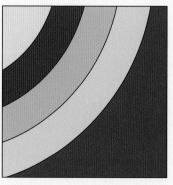

FIGURE 13

If curves aren't your strong suit, an improv block like this one is a stress-free method for piecing curved shapes. —Katy

stepping stones

by TACHA BRUECHER

CUTTING

note: *In addition to fabric, you will need a 12½-inch (31.8 cm) square of freezer paper and fusible web.*

1 From assorted fabrics, cut the following:
- ☐ For the center strip behind the circles, one rectangle measuring 5½ x 18½ inches (14 x 47 cm)
- ☐ 2 strips of yellow measuring 1 x 14 inches (2.5 x 35.6 cm)
- ☐ Other strips of varying widths x 12½ inches (31.8 cm)
- ☐ 3 squares measuring 3½ inches (8.9 cm)

ASSEMBLY

2 On the dull side of the 12½-inch (31.8 cm) square of freezer paper, mark a point 3½ inches (3.5 cm) from the top right-hand corner on both the top and side edges. Do the same on the bottom left-hand corner. Join the points to make a wide strip across the diagonal of the square **(FIGURE 14)**.

3 Position the center fabric strip over the diagonal lines with the wrong side of the fabric facing the shiny side of freezer paper. Press in place. Stitch the yellow strips through the paper on both sides of the central strip (page 134) **(FIGURE 15)**.

4 One at a time, add strips of varying widths and at different angles to the yellow strips on both sides, until the freezer paper is covered **(FIGURE 16)**. Stitch these strips through the fabric only; do not sew through the paper.

5 Turn the block over and trim it to 12½ inches (31.8 cm), using the freezer paper as a guide. Remove the freezer paper.

6 Draw three circles with a 3½-inch (8.9 cm) diameter on the fusible web. Cut them out slightly outside the lines and fuse them to the wrong side of the remaining fabric squares, following manufacturer's directions. Cut out the fabric circles and fuse them to the diagonal brown strip. Stitch around the edge of each circle to secure.

FIGURE 14

FIGURE 15

FIGURE 16

joseph's coat
by BRIONI GREENBERG

CUTTING

note: *In addition to fabric, you will also need a 6 x 12-inch (15.2 x 30.5 cm) piece of fusible web and template plastic.*

1 From assorted green background prints, cut the following:
- ☐ 6 squares measuring 6½ inches (16.5 cm)
- ☐ 4 rectangles measuring 3¾ x 7 inches (9.5 x 17.8 cm)
- ☐ 2 rectangles measuring 1¾ x 8 inches (4.4x 20.3 cm)

2 From assorted pink petal prints, cut 12 rectangles measuring 1⅓ x 6½ inches (3.4 x 16.5 cm).

3 Enlarge the templates (A, B, C, and the petal shape) on page 138. Trace them onto template plastic and cut them out. Label each template on the wrong side.

4 Trace the templates on the wrong side of the green background fabrics as listed and cut them out:
- ☐ Template A on the 6½-inch (16.5 cm) squares.
- ☐ Template B on the 1¾ x 8-inch (4.4 x 20.3 cm) rectangles.
- ☐ Template C on two of the 3¾ x 7-inch (9.5 x 17.8 cm) rectangles; flip the template over and trace it on the remaining green rectangles to form mirror images.

ASSEMBLY

5 Lay out the template pieces **(FIGURE 17)**, and stitch them together:
- ☐ Start by stitching each of the template A pieces to either a template B or C piece. Press the seams open to reduce bulk.
- ☐ Stitch three sections together for the left-hand side, then the remaining three sections for the right-hand side. Stitch the two halves together and press seams open.

6 Trace the petal template eight times on the paper side of the fusible web and cut out the shapes outside the drawn lines. Press these to the wrong side of the petal fabric, following the manufacturer's instructions. Cut out the shapes along the drawn lines.

7 Use the diagram as a guide to layout the petals on the block, covering all seams **(FIGURE 18)**. Peel off the paper side of the web and press the petal shapes in place. Stitch around the edge of each petal appliqué to secure.

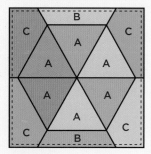

FIGURE 17

FIGURE 18

convergence

by JOHN Q. ADAMS

CUTTING

1 Cut a total of eight squares measuring 8½ inches (21.6 cm), as follows:

- ☐ 2 from raspberry fabric
- ☐ 2 from a different raspberry fabric
- ☐ 2 from a brown fabric
- ☐ 2 from a yellow fabric

- -

ASSEMBLY

2 With all fabrics right side up, stack two matching raspberry print squares atop the two brown squares, aligning all of the corners. Select two circle templates of your choosing, one slightly larger than the other. Make two curved cuts through the stack of squares, as seen in the finished block.

tip: *Circular items like CDs, plates, and mug rims make great templates. The size is not important, as long as you use the same two templates for all cuts.*

3 Take one inner (quarter-circle) piece from the raspberry fabric and join it with a brown middle piece. Pin and stitch together along the curve. Press well. Join this piece with an outer cut of the raspberry background fabric. Trim the block to 6½ inches (16.5 cm) square. Repeat to make a second identical block.

4 Repeat steps 2 and 3, using the remaining two raspberry squares and the two yellow squares.

note: *You will have leftover pieces to make contrasting blocks to use in your quilt, or in another project.*

5 Join the quadrants together as shown in the photo. Press.

For this circle block, I decided to not include a circle at all! Rather, my design blows the circle apart and rearranges its four quadrants. The power of this design comes in its repeat: imagine a quilt featuring this block in a tiled design.

— *John*

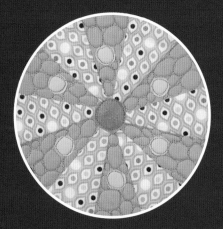

satellite placemats

by Brioni Greenberg ■ finished size of each placemat: approximately
15½ inches (39.4 cm) in diameter

These placemats combine fun wedge shapes and raw-
edge appliqué for a design that is just large enough to
peek out from beneath a plate of your favorite home-
cooked meal. These instructions make four placemats.

materials

- ☐ 1 fat quarter of solid tan fabric
- ☐ 1 fat quarter of print fabric
- ☐ ½ yard (.5 m) of green solid fabric for borders
- ☐ ½ yard (.5 m) of white or cream solid fabric for binding
- ☐ 1 yard (.9 m) of fabric for backing
- ☐ 4 pieces of batting at least 18 inches (45.7 cm) square
- ☐ Templates (page 139)
- ☐ Fabric scraps for appliqué circles
- ☐ Clear template plastic
- ☐ Fusible web

cutting

1 Cut 12 rectangles measuring 4 x 7 inches (10.2 x 17.8 cm) from both fat quarters, for a total of 24 rectangles.

2 Cut all rectangles in half diagonally. Reshape each of the resulting triangles by making one cut from the top left-hand corner to a line 1 inch (2.5 cm) down from the top on the right-hand side **(FIGURE 19)**.

3 From the green border fabric, cut 48 rectangles measuring 2 x 5 inches (5.1 x 12.7 cm).

4 From the backing fabric, cut four squares measuring 18 inches (45.7 cm). You can do this by cutting the yard of fabric into four pieces of equal size.

5 From the white binding fabric, cut seven strips measuring 2½ inches (6.4 cm) x the width of the fabric.

6 Enlarge the templates on page 139. Trace them onto template plastic and cut them out.

assembly

7 Stitch a green border rectangle to the top of each of the 48 wedges. Press open. Trim the edges of each border to match the angle of the sides **(FIGURE 20)**.

8 For each placemat, you will need 12 wedges: six from the solid fabric and six from the print fabric. Lay out the wedges so the pieces alternate between solid and print, and stitch them together in quarters. Sew the quarters together to form four placemats.

9 Adhere fusible web to the fabric scraps, following the manufacturer's instructions, and use the templates to cut out the following four times for a set of four placemats:

   ☐ 6 circles from template A
   ☐ 7 circles from template B
   ☐ 6 circles from template C

In the example, each template size is cut from the same fabric color except for one template B circle, which is cut from a different color for the center.

10 Remove the paper backing from each of the circles and arrange the pieces on the solid fabric wedges as follows:

   ☐ Place template A circles 2 inches (5.1 cm) from the center of the placemat.
   ☐ Place template B circles 4 inches (10.2 cm) from the center of the placemat.

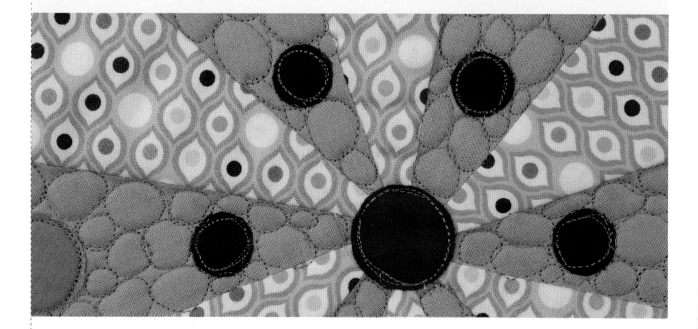

☐ Place template C circles 6 inches (15.2 cm) from the center of the placemat.

☐ Place the remaining template B circle in the very center of the placemat.

☐ Once you are happy with the placement, press to adhere it to the backing.

11 Make a quilt sandwich with the backing, batting, and placemat tops. Baste the pieces together.

12 Start quilting from the center and work your way out to the edges. In the example, a pebble pattern was quilted on the solid wedges and alternating border rectangles. As you reach each circle, stitch it down around all the edges. You may want to stitch around twice.

13 Trim the edges of each placement 1½ inches (3.8 cm) from the green border seam.

14 Stitch the binding strips end to end to make one long strip. Bind the placemats (page 137) and enjoy!

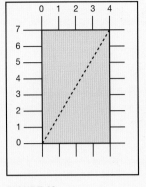

FIGURE 19

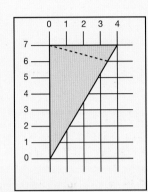

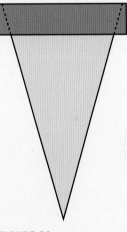

FIGURE 20

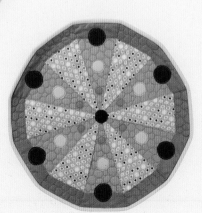

orange soda quilt

by Katy Jones ■ finished size: 69 x 85 inches (175.3x 215.9 cm), twin size ■ machine quilting by Christine Marriage using "Bubble Play" by Vickie Malaski of Designs by Vickie

Not all circles in quilting need to be made using curved seams. Orange Soda is a modern play on the traditional blocks named Orange Peel and Robbing Peter to Pay Paul. The background is constructed using the simplest of patchwork, and the fused appliqué petal shapes give the illusion of circles.

materials

- ☐ Total of 5 yards (4.6 m) of fabric for background squares, from at least 15 different fabrics (the greater the variety, the more vibrant your quilt will be)
- ☐ 4 yards (3.7 m) of a contrasting solid or pin dot fabric for appliquéd petal shapes and binding
- ☐ 5½ yards (5m) of fabric for backing
- ☐ 1 piece of batting, 75 x 90 inches (190.5 x 228.6cm)
- ☐ 9 yards (8.2 m) of 12-inch-wide (30.5 cm) fusible web, or 36 of the 8 x 12-inch (20.3 x 30.5 cm) sheets
- ☐ Template plastic
- ☐ Large petal template (page 139)

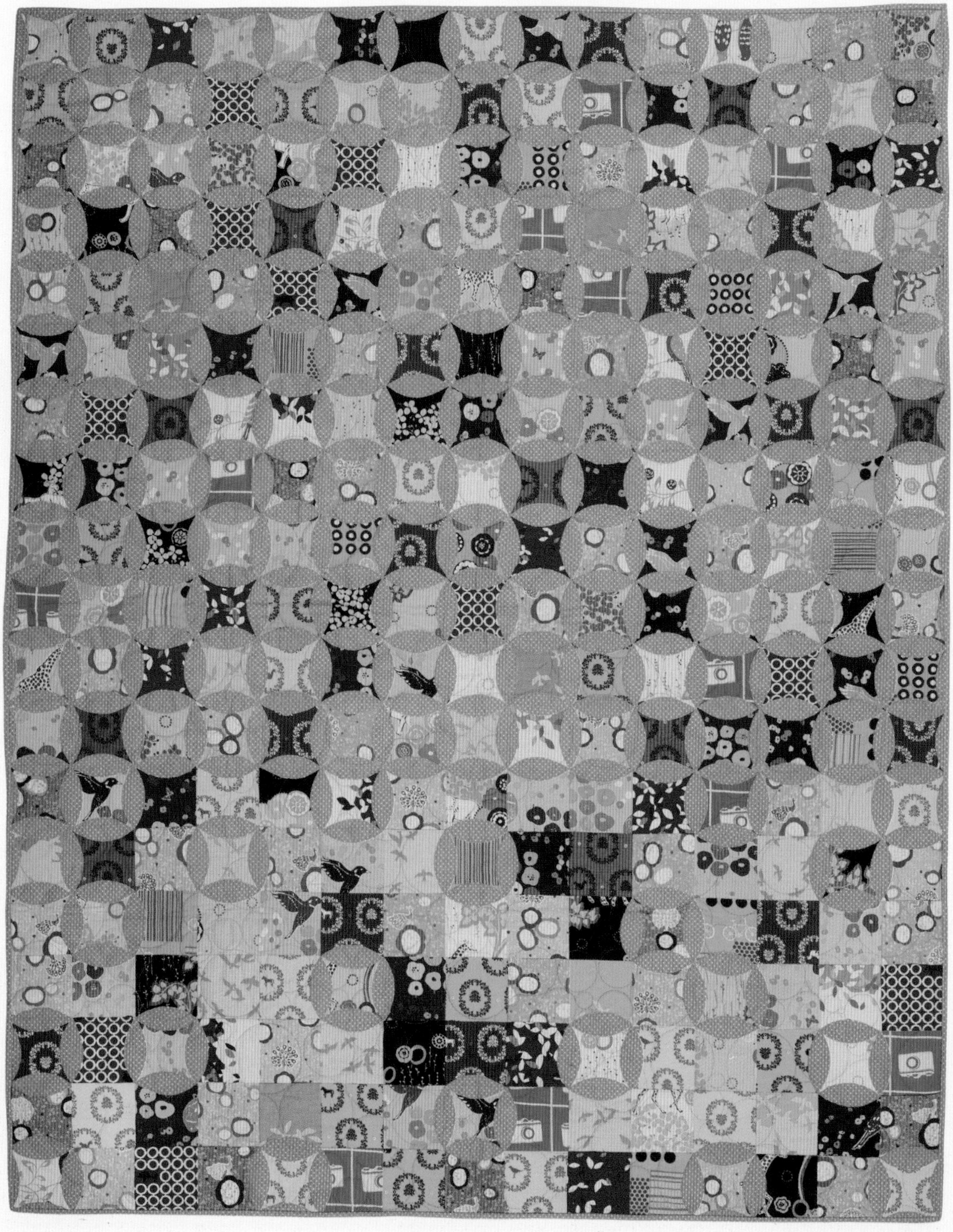

cutting

1 From the background fabric, cut 285 squares measuring 5 inches (12.7 cm).

2 Enlarge the petal template, trace it onto template plastic, and cut it out. Trace the template on the paper side of the fusible web to make a total of 420 full petal shapes. Leave a bit of space outside each shape. Also trace an additional 25 petal shapes and cut them in half lengthwise to make 50 half-petal shapes. (You will use 49.)

3 Follow the manufacturer's instructions to adhere the shapes to the wrong side of the contrasting solid fabric. Cut out the fabric pieces and set them aside.

4 Cut the remaining solid fabric into 2½-inch-wide (6.4 cm) strips and sew them together end-to-end to make one long binding strip. You will need approximately 325 inches (825.5 cm) for binding (or 8 strips of 42-inch-wide [106.7 cm] fabric).

assembly

5 To sew the background:
- ☐ Arrange the 5-inch (12.7 cm) squares in 19 rows of 15 squares. Play around with the layout to ensure you don't have two of the same fabrics too close together.
- ☐ Stack each row from left to right and pin a note on top with the number of the row.
- ☐ Stitch the squares together to make each row.
- ☐ Stitch the rows together.
- ☐ Press the seams open to reduce bulk.
- ☐ Stitch around the whole perimeter of the background using a ⅛-inch (3 mm) seam allowance. This will stabilize the quilt top; you'll be moving it around a lot as you attach the appliqués and the edges of the top can come unraveled if not secured.

6 Peel the paper backing off the petals and arrange them on top of the seams, as done in the quilt block on page 33. Work from the top of the quilt top down, and press one row of petal shapes at a time.

7 Choose a thread that matches the appliqué fabric, and stitch the petals in place across the rows **(FIGURE 21)**. Follow the arrows in one direction, then turn and stitch in the reverse direction back across the row. The appliqués in this quilt were free-motion stitched (page 133), but a zigzag or blanket stitch will work just as well.

8 Refer to pages 135–137 for help with basting, quilting, and binding.

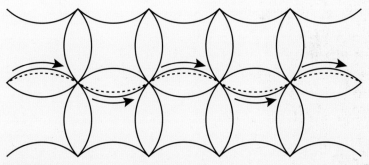

FIGURE 21

triangles

THE TRIANGLE IS A CLOSED, three-sided shape with sides that are the same or differing lengths. Any shape with three points that can be connected by straight lines is a triangle. And of all the shapes in quilting, triangles are perhaps the most versatile. The humble half-square triangle, a square cut in half across the bias (page 131), is used for a striking effect in a number of ways in this chapter. You can also experiment with adding squares or rectangles, and using different sizes of half-square triangles in the same block.

From basic triangles, you can move to impressive projects such as Fast Forward/Rewind Quilt (page 64), a quilt that uses triangles to create a sense of movement. Or how about mixing up the traditional square log cabin block and using a triangle at the center?

Triangles are not to be feared! Embrace them, master them, and they will soon become a favorite in your skills arsenal.

triangle tumbler

by TACHA BRUECHER

CUTTING

note: *In addition to fabric, you will also need template plastic and fusible web.*

1 Enlarge the templates on page 139. Trace them onto template plastic and label them A, B, C, and D.

2 From both a green solid and a green print, cut out the following:
- ☐ 2 of template A
- ☐ 2 of template D

3 From both a white solid and a blue print, cut 2 of template B.

4 From a gray solid, cut 4 of template C.

- -

ASSEMBLY

5 To complete each quarter-block **(FIGURE 1)**:
- ☐ Stitch the gray template C pieces to the right-hand side of each template A triangle.
- ☐ On the left-hand side of the green solid triangles, stitch the white template B pieces.
- ☐ On the left-hand side of the green print triangles, stitch the blue template B pieces.
- ☐ Trim the blocks to 6½ inches (16.5 cm) square.

6 Trace template D onto the paper side of fusible web four timest. Fuse to the wrong side of the template D fabric pieces following the manufacturer's directions. Cut out the fabric triangles, peel off the paper backing, and fuse them to the center of each template A triangle. Stitch to secure in place.

7 Arrange the finished triangle blocks as shown **(FIGURE 2)** and stitch them together.

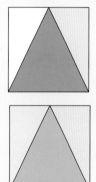

FIGURE 1

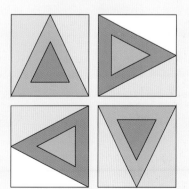

FIGURE 2

migration

by JOHN Q. ADAMS

CUTTING

1 From assorted fabric scraps, cut out the following pieces:

- ☐ red solid, 1 square measuring 3⅞ inches (9.8 cm)
- ☐ leaf print, 1 square measuring 6⅞ inches (17.5 cm)
- ☐ red print, 2 squares measuring 3⅞ inches (9.8 cm)
- ☐ green print, 4 squares measuring 3⅞ inches (9.8 cm)
- ☐ light gray solid, 4 rectangles measuring 3½ x 6½ inches (8.9 x 16.5 cm)

2 Cut all of the squares in half on the diagonal.

ASSEMBLY

3 Assemble the block according to the diagram **(FIGURE 3)**. You will have extra triangles left over.

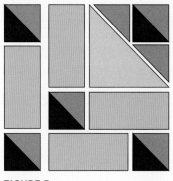

FIGURE 3

points practice

by KATY JONES

CUTTING

1 Cut three squares measuring 4 inches (10.2 cm) from each of the following fabrics:

- ☐ blue print #1
- ☐ blue print #2
- ☐ green print #1
- ☐ green print #2
- ☐ white print
- ☐ red solid

2 Cut each square in half diagonally to make two triangles from each square.

- -

ASSEMBLY

3 Refer to the photo for layout and pairing of triangles.

4 Stitch each pair of triangles together to form squares, making sure you don't stretch or distort them. Press seams open to reduce bulk, and trim.

5 Stitch the squares together in rows, and then stitch the rows together. In order to achieve well-matched points, ensure the seams of each square are nestled together and pinned well. A good tip is to pin in the middle where the seams match, and at each edge— a total of three pins each time.

If you're a beginner quilter, perfect points can seem a bit tricky. Half-square triangles like the ones in this block are a great way to practice. Try cutting your initial squares a little larger, and then trim down each half-square triangle unit before you sew them into a block.
— Katy

x marks the spot

by BRIONI GREENBERG

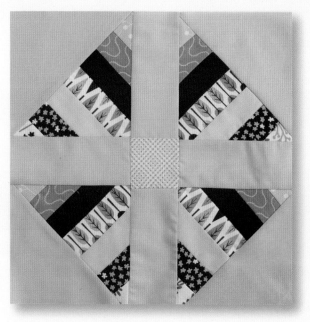

CUTTING

1 From each of 7 scrap fabrics, cut the following:
- ☐ 2 strips measuring 1½ x 8½ inches (3.8 x 21.6 cm)

2 From one of the lighter scraps, cut:
- ☐ 1 square measuring 2½ inches (6.4 cm)

3 From gray solid (background) fabric, cut the following:
- ☐ 2 squares measuring 6 inches (15.2 cm)
- ☐ 4 strips measuring 2½ x 5½ inches (6.4 x 14 cm)

4 From paper, cut two squares measuring 6 inches (15.2 cm).

ASSEMBLY

5 Use the foundation piecing method (page 134) to make the featured triangles. (Remember to reduce your stitch length to make it easier to remove the papers later.)
- ☐ Place a strip, right side up, diagonally across the center of one of the paper squares.
- ☐ Place the next strip, right side down, and line the edge up with the first strip.
- ☐ Stitch a seam ¼ inch (.6 cm) from the edges.
- ☐ Continue sewing strips until the whole paper is covered.
- ☐ Make a second pieced square using the same method.
- ☐ Trim the blocks to 6 inches (15.2 cm) square and remove the papers from the back of each square.

6 Make four half-square triangles (page 131) using the two pieced squares and two gray squares. Trim the half square triangles to 5½ inches (14 cm).

7 Use the diagram as a guide to assemble and stitch the block **(FIGURE 4)**.

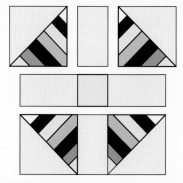

FIGURE 4

I love how string blocks look, but I haven't always got the patience to sew block after block of strips. This was the start of an experiment in making string blocks and then chopping them up to create something else.

— *Brioni*

meeting point

by TACHA BRUECHER

CUTTING

1 From assorted fabrics, cut out the following pieces:
- □ blue print, 12 squares measuring 2½ inches (6.4 cm)
- □ green print #1, 4 rectangles measuring 2½ x 4½ inches (6.4 x 11.4 cm)
- □ green print #2, 4 rectangles measuring 2½ x 4½ inches (6.4 x 11.4 cm)

2 From dark green solid fabric, cut:
- □ 2 rectangles measuring 2½ x 4½ inches (6.4 x 11.4 cm)
- □ 2 squares measuring 5 inches (12.7 cm)

3 From white solid fabric, cut:
- □ 2 squares measuring 5 inches (12.7 cm)
- □ 8 squares measuring 2½ inches (6.4 cm)

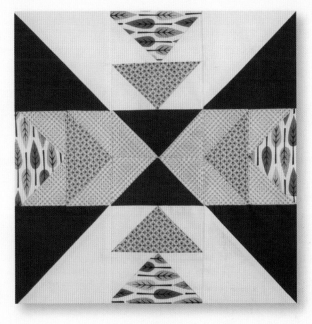

ASSEMBLY

4 Make four half-square triangles (page 131) using the 5-inch (12.7 cm) dark green and white solid squares.

5 Make six flying geese units (page 131) using the 12 blue squares and the following 2½ x 4½-inch (6.4 x 11.4 cm) rectangles:
- □ 2 of green print #1
- □ 2 of green print #2
- □ 2 of dark green

6 Make four flying geese units using the eight white squares and the remaining green rectangles.

7 Follow the diagram **(FIGURE 5)** to assemble and stitch the block.

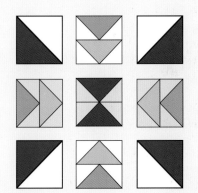

FIGURE 5

bowties & blooms

by JOHN Q. ADAMS

CUTTING

1 Cut out the following from assorted fabric scraps as listed:

- ☐ salmon solid, 2 squares measuring 3⅞ inches (9.8 cm)
- ☐ blue floral print, 1 square measuring 3⅞ inches (9.8 cm)
- ☐ blue tree print, 1 square measuring 6⅞ inches (17.5 cm)

2 From gray solid fabric, cut:

- ☐ 4 squares measuring 3½ inches (8.9cm)
- ☐ 5 squares measuring 3⅞ inches (9.8 cm)

3 Cut all the squares, except for the gray 3½-inch (8.9 cm) squares, in half on the diagonal.

- -

ASSEMBLY

4 Assemble the pieces based on the diagram **(FIGURE 6)**. Stitch together each quadrant, then stitch those together.

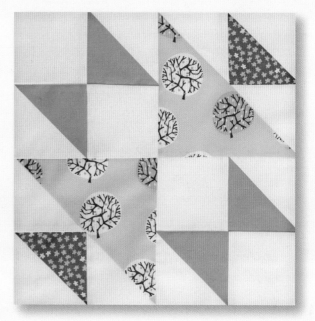

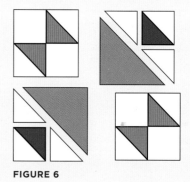

FIGURE 6

fleeing the nest

by BRIONI GREENBERG

CUTTING

note: *In addition to fabric, you will also need template plastic.*

1 Enlarge the templates on page 139. Trace each one onto template plastic and label it with the correct letter.

note: *Template A is not an equilateral triangle, so be sure to mark the bottom of the template and the bottom of the fabrics when cutting them out (a small X in the seam allowance should do the trick).*

2 Select four assorted print fabrics for the triangles. The innermost triangle in the block will be fabric #1, the next fabric #2, and so on. From fabric #1, cut the following:
- ☐ 4 of template A
- ☐ 2 squares measuring 2½ inches (6.4cm), then cut in half diagonally to make four triangles

3 From each of fabrics #2 and #3, cut four of template A.

4 From fabric #4, cut two squares measuring 2¾ inches (7 cm), then cut them in half diagonally to make four triangles.

5 From red solid fabric, cut:
- ☐ 1 of template C
- ☐ 12 of template B
- ☐ 12 of template B reversed

6 From white solid fabric, cut two squares measuring 7 inches (17.8 cm), and cut them in half diagonally to make four triangles.

- -

ASSEMBLY

7 Stitch two red template B pieces (1 reversed) to both sides of each template A fabric triangle to make a total of 12 blocks.

8 Assemble four strips, each with three blocks; keep the fabrics in order, with fabric #1 at the bottom of each strip.

9 Using the diagram as a guide **(FIGURE 7)**, stitch the separate pieces together to form the block.

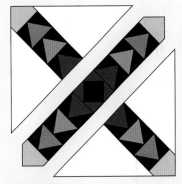

FIGURE 7

landscape

by TACHA BRUECHER

CUTTING

1 From assorted fabrics, cut the following pieces:
- □ green print, 8 rectangles measuring 2½ x 4½ inches (6.4 x 11.4cm)
- □ blue print #1, 8 squares measuring 2½ inches (6.4 cm)
- □ white solid, 8 squares measuring 2½ inches (6.4 cm)
- □ blue print #2, 3 rectangles measuring 3½ x 6½ inches (8.9 x 16.5 cm)
- □ dark green solid, 6 squares measuring 3½ inches (8.9 cm)

2 From medium green solid, cut:
- □ 1 rectangle measuring 1½ x 4½ inches (1.5 x 11.4 cm)
- □ 1 rectangle measuring 2½ x 3½ inches (6.4 x 3.5cm)
- □ 1 rectangle measuring 2½ x 4½ inches (6.4 x 11.4 cm)
- □ 2 squares measuring 2½ inches (6.4 cm)

ASSEMBLY

3 Make the eight smaller flying geese units (page 131) using the green print rectangles and the blue and white squares.

4 Make the three larger flying geese units using the blue print rectangles and dark green squares.

5 Arrange the top portion of the block with the following pieces **(FIGURE 8)**, and stitch them together:
- □ 1 large flying geese unit
- □ 4 small flying geese units
- □ the first two medium green rectangles listed in step 2

6 Arrange the bottom left portion of the block with the following pieces **(FIGURE 9)**, and stitch them together:
- □ 1 large flying geese unit
- □ 2 small flying geese units
- □ the third medium green rectangle listed in step 2

7 Arrange the bottom right portion of the block with the following pieces **(FIGURE 10)**, and stitch them together:
- □ 1 large flying geese unit
- □ 2 small flying geese units
- □ the remaining medium green squares

8 Stitch the units together as shown **(FIGURE 11)**.

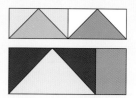

FIGURE 8

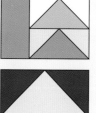
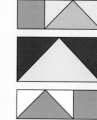

FIGURE 9   **FIGURE 10**

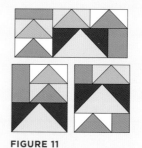

FIGURE 11

pyramid scheme

by JOHN Q. ADAMS

CUTTING

1 From each of the following fabrics, cut two squares measuring 3 inches (7.6 cm).

☐ green solid
☐ green print #1
☐ green print #2

2 From green print #2, also cut 1 square measuring 5⅛ inches (13 cm).

3 From gray solid fabric, cut:

☐ 6 squares measuring 3 inches (7.6 cm)
☐ 1 square measuring 5⅛ inches (13 cm)
☐ 2 squares measuring 6⅞ inches (17.5 cm)

- -

ASSEMBLY

4 Make 10 half-square triangles (page 131) by pairing the 3-inch (7.6 cm) gray squares with the green solid and print squares of the same size.

5 Cut all the other squares in half diagonally. You will use only one half of the 5⅛-inch (13 cm) squares in the construction of this block.

6 Assemble the block according to the diagrams **(FIGURES 12-14)**.

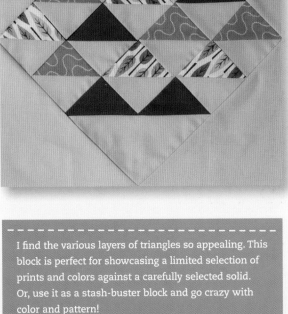

I find the various layers of triangles so appealing. This block is perfect for showcasing a limited selection of prints and colors against a carefully selected solid. Or, use it as a stash-buster block and go crazy with color and pattern!

— John

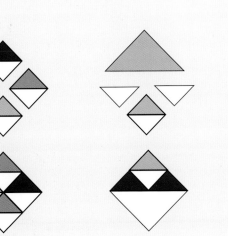

FIGURE 12

FIGURE 13

FIGURE 14

zigzags
by KATY JONES

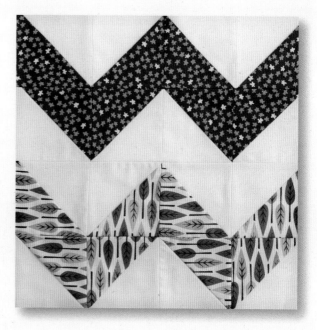

CUTTING

1 From each of two different print fabrics, cut four squares measuring 4 inches (10.2 cm), for a total of 8 squares.

2 From solid background fabric, cut eight squares measuring 4 inches (10.2 cm).

- -

ASSEMBLY

3 Make 16 half-square triangles (page 131) by pairing each of the 8 background squares with a print square.

4 Follow the diagram to arrange the blocks **(FIGURE 15)**. Stitch the blocks together in rows, then stitch the rows together. Press the seams open.

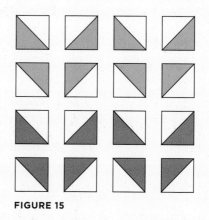

FIGURE 15

floating triangles wall hanging

by Katy Jones ■ finished size: 18 x 24 inches (45.7 x 61 cm)

This fun mini-quilt is an ideal way to showcase some of your most treasured scraps. The technique is fast and simple, and would look stunning as a full quilt using different fabrics for each background.

materials

- ☐ Assorted small fabric scraps for the triangles
- ☐ 12 assorted scraps measuring 3 x 18 inches (7.6 x 45.7cm) for the small background squares
- ☐ ¾ yard (1.9 m) of background fabric
- ☐ 1 piece of batting, 20 x 26 inches (50.8 x 66 cm)
- ☐ ¾ yard (1.9 m) of backing fabric
- ☐ 95-inch (241.3 cm) length of binding

cutting

1 From the small fabric scraps, cut:
- ☐ 12 squares measuring 1 inch (2.5 cm) for the triangle centers
- ☐ 24 strips measuring between ½ and 1 inch (1.3 and 2.5 cm) wide and approximately 4 inches (10.2 cm) in length for two rows around each triangle center

2 Cut each of the 12 assorted 3 x 18-inch (7.6 x 45.7cm) scraps into three strips measuring 3 x 6 inches (7.6 x 15.2 cm).

3 Cut the background fabric into strips measuring 3 inches (7.6 cm) x the width of the fabric. Cross-cut these strips into the following lengths:
- ☐ 12 strips that are 4½ inches (11.4 cm) long
- ☐ 24 strips that are 8 inches (20.3 cm) long
- ☐ 12 strips that are 12 inches (30.5 cm) long

- -

assembly

4 Cut each 1-inch (2.5 cm) square scrap into a rough triangle shape. Using a log cabin method, stitch three scrap strips around each center triangle and trim the ends as needed **(FIGURE 16)**.

5 Repeat with a second row of scrap strips. Keep trimming into a triangle shape as necessary.

6 Stitch the inner background strips in a log cabin style around each triangle **(FIGURE 17)**.

7 Using a rotary cutter and mat, convert the triangles into 4½-inch (11.4 cm) squares **(FIGURE 18)**. Make a total of 12 blocks.

8 Stitch the background strips to each square as follows, to form 6½-inch (16.5 cm) blocks:
- ☐ Stitch the 4½-inch (11.4 cm) strips to the top of each block.
- ☐ Stitch 8-inch (21.6cm) strips on one side and the bottom of each block.
- ☐ Finish with a 12-inch (30.5 cm) strip on the remaining side of each block.

9 Cut each square so that the inner block appears wonky.

10 Stitch the blocks into four rows of three blocks.

11 Refer to pages 135–137 for tips on basting, quilting, and binding your quilt.

FIGURE 16

FIGURE 17

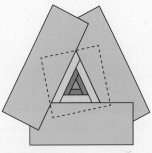

FIGURE 18

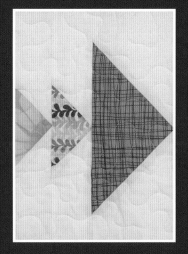

 fast forward/rewind quilt

by Tacha Bruecher ▪ finished size: 61 x 84 inches (154.9 x 213.4 cm)

Don't be put off by the number of geese in this stunning quilt. Cut all the fabric first, chain piece the flying geese, and you will be done in a jiffy!

materials

☐ 3 fat eighths of different orange prints
☐ 6 fat quarters of different green prints
☐ 6 fat eighths of different yellow prints
☐ 3 fat eighths of different gray prints
☐ 2 yards (1.8 m) of linen
☐ 4½ yards (4.1 m) of white solid
☐ ⅝ yard (.6 m) of binding fabric
☐ Piece of batting, 70 x 92 inches (177.8 x 233.7 cm)
☐ 5 yards (4.6 m) of backing fabric

cutting

1 From green, yellow, orange, and gray prints, cut a total of:

- ☐ 48 rectangles measuring 2½ x 4½ inches (6.4 x 11.4 cm)
- ☐ 24 rectangles measuring 3½ x 6½ inches (8.9 x 16.5 cm)
- ☐ 18 rectangles measuring 4½ x 8½ inches (11.4 x 21.6 cm)
- ☐ 12 rectangles measuring 5½ x 10½ inches (14 x 26.7 cm)

2 From white solid fabric, cut:

- ☐ 96 rectangles measuring 2½ x 6½ inches (6.4 x 16.5 cm)
- ☐ 48 rectangles measuring 3½ x 6½ inches (8.9 x 16.5 cm)
- ☐ 36 rectangles measuring 4½ x 6½ inches (11.4 x 16.5 cm)
- ☐ 24 rectangles measuring 5½ x 6½ inches (14 x 16.5 cm)
- ☐ 36 strips measuring 1½ x 6½ inches (3.8 x 16.5 cm)
- ☐ 12 strips measuring 4½ x 12½ inches (11.4 x 31.8 cm)
- ☐ 6 rectangles measuring 1½ x 2½ inches (3.8 x 6.4 cm)

3 From linen fabric, cut:

- ☐ 6 strips measuring 1½ x 12½ inches (3.8x 31.8 cm)
- ☐ 18 rectangles measuring 1½ x 2½ inches (3.8 x 6.4 cm)
- ☐ 12 squares measuring 1½ inches (3.8 cm)
- ☐ 4 strips measuring 1¾ x 6½ inches (4.4 x 16.5 cm)
- ☐ 2 strips measuring 2½ x 4 inches (6.4 x10.2 cm)
- ☐ 2 strips measuring 4 x 53½ inches (10.2 x 135.9 cm)
- ☐ 5 strips measuring 1½ x 61½ inches (3.8 x 156.2 cm)

4 From binding fabric, cut:

- ☐ 8 strips measuring 2½ inches (6.4 cm) x the width of the fabric

assembly

5 Flying geese are made with a fabric rectangle in the center and a fabric square on both ends (page 131), but in this project, all three pieces are rectangles. Here's how you make them:

- ☐ Place the print rectangle face up and line up the white rectangle along one edge, perpendicular to the background fabric.
- ☐ Make a mark on the outside edge of the white solid where the print fabric ends. Draw a line from the top inside corner to the mark on the white solid and stitch along this line **(FIGURE 19)**.
- ☐ Trim to leave a ¼-inch (6 mm) seam allowance, open, and press. Repeat for the other side of the print fabric rectangle **(FIGURE 20)**.

6 Make the flying geese from the following fabric combinations:

- ☐ 48 print 2½ x 4½-inch (6.4x 11.4 cm) rectangles and 96 white 2½ x 6½-inch (6.4 x 16.5 cm) rectangles
- ☐ 24 print 3½ x 6½-inch (8.9 x 16.5cm) rectangles and 48 white 3½ x 6½-inch (8.9 x 16.5 cm) rectangles
- ☐ 18 print 4½ x 8½-inch (11.4 x 21.6 cm) rectangles and 36 white 4½ x 6½-inch (11.4 x 16.5 cm) rectangles
- ☐ 12 print 5½ x 10½-inch (14 x 26.7 cm) rectangles and 24 white 5½ x 6½-inch (14 x16.5 cm) rectangles

7 Sort the geese into six piles, with the following in each pile:

- ☐ 8 geese measuring 2½ inches (6.4 cm) wide
- ☐ 4 geese measuring 3½ inches (8.9 cm) wide
- ☐ 3 geese measuring 4½ inches (11.4 cm) wide
- ☐ 2 geese measuring 5½ inches (14 cm) wide

8 Arrange and stitch each group into a strip measuring 12½ x 50½ inches (128.3 x 156.2 cm). Stitch the linen 1½ x 12½-inch (3.8 x 31.8 cm) strips to the end of each of these strips with the geese pointing towards the linen strip **(FIGURE 21)**.

9 For the smaller blocks at alternating ends of each row:

- ☐ Make 18 flying geese using the linen 1½ x 2½-inch (3.8 x 6.4 cm) rectangles and the 36 white 1½ x 6½-inch (3.8 x 16.5 cm) strips.
- ☐ Stitch these geese together in six groups of three.
- ☐ Stitch a white 4½ x 12½-inch (11.4 x 31.8 cm) strip to both sides of each of these groups.

10 Stitch the linen geese blocks to the print geese strips so that the geese are going in opposite directions **(FIGURE 21)**.

11 To make the end strips for the top and bottom of the quilt **(FIGURE 22)**:

- ☐ Make six flying geese using the white 1½ x 2½-inch (3.8 x 6.4 cm) strips and the 12 linen 1½-inch (3.8 cm) squares.
- ☐ Stitch these flying geese into two strips of three geese along their short sides.
- ☐ Stitch a linen 1¾ x 6½-inch (4.4 x 16.5 cm) strip to the top and the bottom of each of these geese strips.
- ☐ Stitch a linen 2½ x 4-inch (6.4 x 10.2 cm) strip to the left of each geese strip and stitch a linen 4 x 53½-inch (10.2 x 135.9 cm) strip to the right.

12 Arrange the geese strips into six rows, rotating the strips each time to alternate the direction of the geese **(FIGURE 23)** Stitch together with the remaining linen 1½ x 61½-inch (3.8 x 156.2 cm) strips between each row. Sew the linen borders to the top and bottom.

13 Refer to page 135-137 for tips on basting, quilting, and binding your quilt.

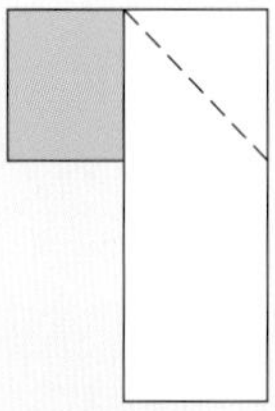

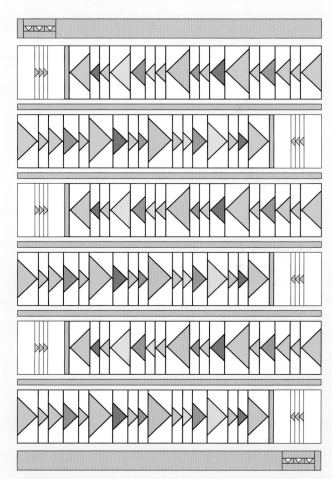

FIGURE 23

FIGURE 19

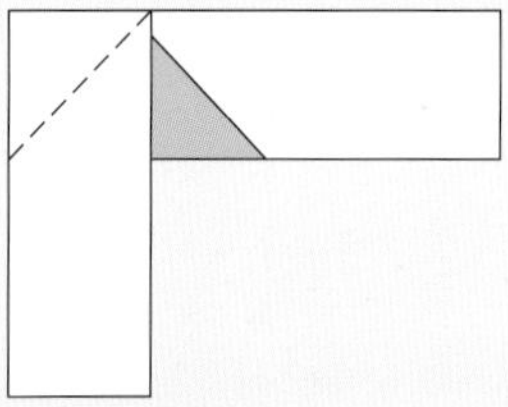

FIGURE 20

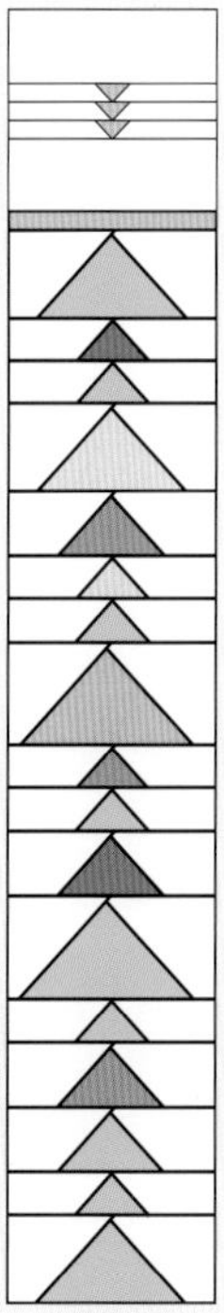

FIGURE 21    **FIGURE 22**

stars

A STAR IS ANY SHAPE with a number of points extending from the center. How many points, and how they are shaped, is up to you.

In quilting terms, a star is most commonly made from a series of triangles around a central square. The simplest stars—even those with just four points—are quick and easy to make, yet very striking. But don't be afraid to tackle more complicated stars too.

Mastering stars is a must. They teach you valuable lessons in fabric placement and composition. You can focus on particular motifs within a fabric and fussy cut them to create stars with interesting centers that are great for baby quilts.

The star shape also lends itself nicely to a variety of piecing techniques. Wonky or precise, paper pieced or appliquéd, there is a star block to suit every project and every taste. Get creative as you incorporate stars in your quilt designs.

Twinkle, twinkle, patchwork star—and just look how versatile you are! Fill your work with a constellation of quilted stars.

spinning star

by JOHN Q. ADAMS

CUTTING

1 Cut two squares measuring 5 inches (12.7 cm) from each of the following fabrics:
- ☐ white solid
- ☐ orange print
- ☐ pink print

2 From focus fabric (for the center), cut:
- ☐ 1 square measuring 4½ inches (11.4 cm)
- ☐ 2 squares measuring 5 inches (12.7 cm)

- -

ASSEMBLY

3 Make four half-square triangles (page 131) using the white and orange squares. Trim them to 4½ inches (11.4 cm).

4 Make four half-square triangles using the pink print and focus print squares. Trim to 4½ inches (11.4cm).

5 Assemble the block as shown (**FIGURE 1**).

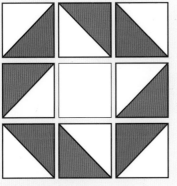

FIGURE 1

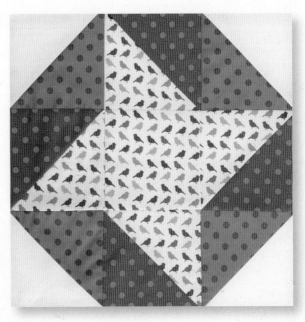

> With this design, I limited myself to very simple and basic block elements—squares and half-square triangles—arranged in a way that creates a contemporary four-pointed star. The limited color palette and careful composition of the colors and prints really helps to modernize this star.
>
> — *John*

patchwork star

by TACHA BRUECHER

CUTTING

1 From white solid fabric, cut one square measuring 12½ inches (31.8 cm).

2 From assorted print fabrics, cut 64 squares measuring 2 inches (5.1 cm).

ASSEMBLY

3 Enlarge the template on page 141 and cut it out. Using a temporary fabric marker, trace the star on the right side of the white solid square. Draw another star inside, about ¼-inch (6 mm) smaller all around. Use scissors to cut out the smaller star, then set this piece aside.

4 Stitch the assorted fabric squares in eight rows of eight squares. Stitch the rows together and press well so the fabric piece lays flat.

5 Place the patchwork piece under the white solid square. Make sure it extends past the cutout star shape by at least ¼ inch (6 mm) in all directions. Pin carefully in place, keeping the two fabric pieces flat against each other.

6 Working on the right side, turn under the white fabric with the tip of your needle as you hand-sew along the marked lines of the large star. Snip into the inside points of the star and trim excess away from the points of the star.

7 Turn the square over and trim the pieced fabric, leaving a ¼-inch (6 mm) seam allowance.

Whether your scrap bucket is overflowing or under control, it's always good to add another scrap buster block to your projects. Sew all those little background bits together, and reverse appliqué all kinds of shapes, like this star.

—Tacha

scrappy star

by KATY JONES

CUTTING

1 From assorted fabrics, cut the following pieces:

☐ green solid, 2 squares measuring 3½ inches (8.9 cm)

☐ pink solid, 2 squares measuring 3½ inches (8.9 cm)

☐ orange print, 2 squares measuring 4 inches (10.2 cm), then cut in half diagonally

☐ pink print, 2 squares measuring 4 inches (10.2 cm), then cut in half diagonally

2 From white solid fabric, cut:

☐ 4 squares measuring 4 inches (10.2 cm), then cut in half diagonally

☐ 4 squares measuring 3½ inches (8.9 cm)

ASSEMBLY

3 Stitch the pink and orange triangles to the white triangles along the diagonal edge, to make a total of eight half-square triangles. Press the seams open and trim to 4 inches (10.2 cm) square.

4 Arrange the blocks as shown (**FIGURE 2**). Stitch them together in rows, then stitch the rows together. Press the seams open.

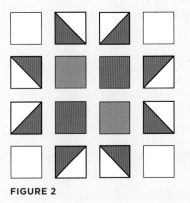

FIGURE 2

twelve-pointed star

by JOHN Q. ADAMS

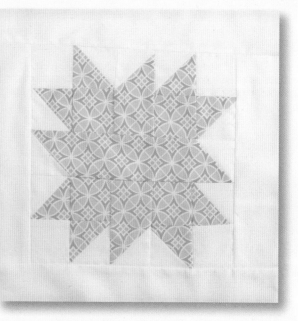

CUTTING

1 From green print fabric, cut:
- ☐ 1 rectangle measuring 2½ x 10½ inches (6.4x 26.7 cm)
- ☐ 2 rectangles measuring 2½ x 4½ inches (6.4 x 11.4 cm)
- ☐ 4 squares measuring 2½ inches (6.4 cm)
- ☐ 4 squares measuring 3 inches (7.6 cm)

2 From white solid fabric, cut:
- ☐ 8 squares measuring 2½ inches (6.4 cm)
- ☐ 4 squares measuring 3 inches (7.6 cm)
- ☐ 2 rectangles measuring 1½ x 10½ inches (3.8 x 26.7 cm)
- ☐ 2 rectangles measuring 1½ x 12½ inches (3.8 x 31.8 cm)

- -

ASSEMBLY

3 Make eight half-square triangles (page 131) using the 3-inch (7.6 cm) white and green print squares.

4 Select four of the 3-inch (7.6 cm) white squares. Draw a faint pencil line across each square.

5 To make the long vertical center strip, align one of the marked white squares with the end of the 2½ x 10½-inch (6.4 x 26.7 cm) green rectangle, positioned as shown **(FIGURE 3)**. Stitch along the line. Trim away the excess fabric, leaving a ¼-inch (6 mm) seam. Press open. Repeat with another white square on the opposite end and diagonally opposite corner of the rectangle.

6 To make the center horizontal cross strips, align the remaining marked white squares with the ends of the 2½ x 4½-inch (6.4 x 11.4 cm) green rectangles **(FIGURE 4)**. Stitch along the lines and trim away the excess fabric as before. Press open.

7 Assemble all of your block components **(FIGURE 5)**. Stitch together in sections as indicated.

FIGURE 3

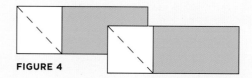

FIGURE 4

FIGURE 5

eight-pointed star

by KATY JONES

CUTTING

1 Cut two squares measuring 4 inches (10.2 cm) from each of the following fabrics:

- ☐ pink print
- ☐ orange print
- ☐ green print
- ☐ yellow print

2 From white solid fabric, cut the following:
- ☐ 4 squares measuring 4 inches (10.2 cm)
- ☐ 4 squares measuring 3½ inches (8.9 cm)

- -

ASSEMBLY

3 Cut all of the 4-inch (10.2 cm) squares in half diagonally.

4 Follow the diagram to arrange the triangles in pairs to form squares **(FIGURE 6)**. Press seams open and trim. Stitch the squares together, row by row, pressing seams open.

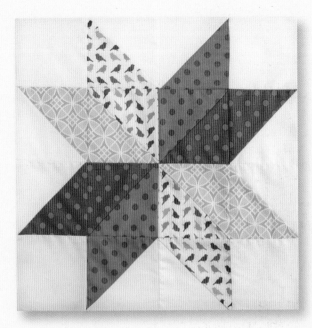

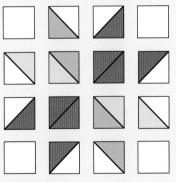

FIGURE 6

Using half-square triangles instead of the more traditional diamond shape is a handy trick for eight-point stars. There are no inset or "Y" seams in this block: you simply sew together a heap of half square triangle units.

— Katy

star within a star

by BRIONI GREENBERG

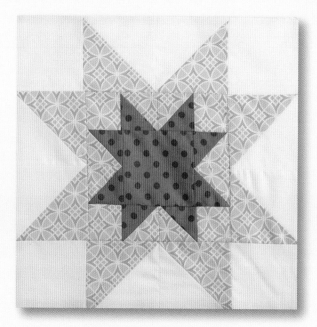

CUTTING

1 From white solid fabric, cut:
- ☐ 4 squares measuring 4 inches (10.2 cm)
- ☐ 4 squares measuring 3½ inches (8.9 cm)

2 From print #1 for the outer star, cut:
- ☐ 4 squares measuring 4 inches (10.2 cm)
- ☐ 4 squares measuring 2½ inches (6.4 cm)
- ☐ 4 squares measuring 2 inches (5.1 cm)

3 From print #2 for the inner star, cut
- ☐ 4 squares measuring 2½ inches (6.4 cm)
- ☐ 1 square measuring 3½ inches (8.9 cm)

- -

ASSEMBLY

4 Make eight half-square triangles (page 131) for the outer star, using the 4-inch (10.2 cm) print #1 squares and white squares. Trim to 3½ inches (8.9 cm).

5 Make eight half-square triangles for the inner star, using the 2½-inch (6.4 cm) print #1 squares and print #2 squares. Trim to 2 inches (5.1 cm).

6 Arrange the smaller blocks to form the inner star **(FIGURE 7)**. Stitch the units together and press.

7 Arrange the remaining half-square triangles around the inner star to form the outer star as seen in the block photo. Stitch the units together and press.

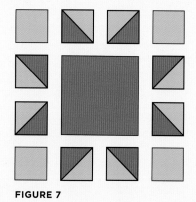

FIGURE 7

three in the breeze

by JOHN Q. ADAMS

CUTTING

1 Cut squares measuring 3½ inches (8.9 cm) from the following fabrics:

- ☐ 1 from pink print
- ☐ 1 from orange print
- ☐ 2 from a focus print

2 From each of red, green, and orange solid fabrics, cut:

- ☐ 2 squares measuring 3 inches (7.6 cm)
- ☐ 4 squares measuring 2½ inches (6.4 cm)

3 From white solid fabric, cut:

- ☐ 6 squares measuring 3 inches (7.6 cm)
- ☐ 3 squares measuring 2½ inches (6.4cm)

ASSEMBLY

4 Stitch the fabric squares listed in step 1 into a four-patch unit, with the focus prints in opposite corners.

5 Make 12 half-square triangles (page 131), using 3-inch (7.6 cm) red, green, and orange solid squares with the same-size white squares. Trim each square to 2½ inches (6.4 cm).

6 Assemble the pieces for each pinwheel block as shown **(FIGURE 8)** and stitch them together.

7 Refer to the black photo to assemble the blocks and stitch them together.

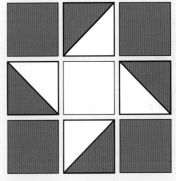

FIGURE 8

paper-pieced star

by TACHA BRUECHER

CUTTING

note: *In addition to the fabric listed, you will need one fat quarter of white solid fabric and freezer paper.*

1 Cut the following pieces for the star:
- ☐ pink print, 5 rectangles measuring 4½ x 3½ inches (11.4 x 8.9 cm)
- ☐ green print, 5 rectangles measuring 3½ x 6½ inches (8.9 x 16.5 cm)

2 Cut the following pieces for the border:
- ☐ orange print, 2 strips measuring 1½ x 12½ inches (3.8 x 31.8 cm)
- ☐ focus print, 2 strips measuring 10½ x 12½ inches (26.7 x 31.8 cm)

ASSEMBLY

3 The block is paper-pieced in 10 sections. Enlarge the templates on page 140 and trace them onto the freezer paper. Transfer the numbers as they appear on the templates to the fabric make assembly easier.

4 Press the pink print pieces to the shiny side of all the odd-numbered spikes. Press the green print pieces to the even-numbered spikes. In each case, make sure the fabric covers the numbered diamond with at least a ¼-inch (6 mm) overhang.

5 Paper piece the unnumbered sections on each blade with white solid fabric from the fat quarter. Keep in mind that the paper pattern templates do NOT include a seam allowance.

6 Trim each section to ¼ inch (.6 cm) larger than the paper pattern **(FIGURE 9)**. Remove the paper.

7 Assemble the star in two halves. Stitch blades 1 through 5 together to form half of the star. Stitch blades 6 through 10 to form the other half **(FIGURE 10)**.

8 Stitch the two halves together. The block should measure 10½ inches (26.7 cm) square.

9 To add the border, stitch the two focal print strips to the sides of the star block. Stitch the strips to the top and bottom of the star block.

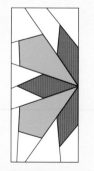 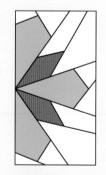

FIGURE 9   FIGURE 10

wonky star nine-patch

by BRIONI GREENBERG

CUTTING

1 From white solid fabric, cut:
- ☐ 4 rectangles measuring 3½ x 5 inches (8.9 x 12.7 cm)
- ☐ 32 squares measuring 2 inches (5.1 cm)

2 Cut the fabric for the points of the small stars from two different fabrics, print #1 and print #2. From each print, cut 8 squares measuring 2½ inches (6.4 cm). Cut each square in half diagonally, for a total of 32 triangles.

3 From print #3, for the points of the large star, cut four rectangles measuring 3 x 4½ inches (7.6 x 11.4 cm). Cut each rectangle in half diagonally to make eight triangles.

4 From print #4, for the center of the stars, cut:
- ☐ 4 squares measuring 2 inches (5.1 cm)
- ☐ 1 square measuring 3½ inches (8.9 cm)

- -

ASSEMBLY

5 To make the points of the small stars:
- ☐ On top of a 2-inch (5.1 cm) white square, position a print #1 triangle right side down as shown **(FIGURE 11)**. Stitch in place. Trim excess fabric from the seam allowance and press open.
- ☐ Repeat the process with another print #1 triangle. Trim excess fabric from the seam allowance and press open **(FIGURE 12)**. Trim the square to 2 inches (5.1 cm).
- ☐ Repeat the process to make a total of 16 pieced triangle units. You will use all 32 print #1 and print #2 triangles.

6 Assemble and stitch four individual stars **(FIGURE 13)**, using the following pieces for each star:
- ☐ 4 pieced triangle units from the same fabric
- ☐ 4 squares measuring 2 inches (5.1 cm)
- ☐ 1 print #4 center square measuring 2 inches (5.1 cm)

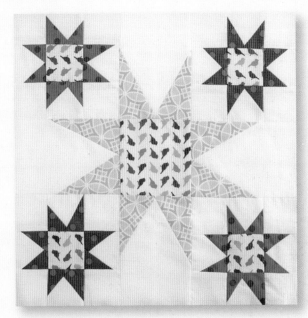

7 Stitch two print #3 triangles to both sides of a 3½ x 5-inch (8.9 x 12.7 cm) white rectangle in the same way as in steps 5 and 6. Repeat to make four pieced triangle units.

8 Assemble and stitch all pieces together, using the block photo as a guide.

FIGURE 11   **FIGURE 12**

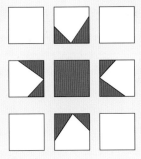

FIGURE 13

star pinwheel

by BRIONI GREENBERG

CUTTING

note: *In addition to fabric, you will need clear template plastic and a piece of fusible web approximately 4½ x 18 inches (11.4 x45.7 cm).*

1 From both white solid fabric and print fabric, cut the following pieces:

☐ 2 squares measuring 7 inches (17.8 cm)

☐ 4 strips measuring 2½ x 4½ inches (6.4 x 11.4 cm)

- -

ASSEMBLY

2 Make four half-square triangles (page 131) using the white and print squares. Press and trim to 6½ inches (16.5 cm) square.

3 Arrange these squares together so that the print triangles form a pinwheel shape. Stitch the squares together into a block and press seams open.

4 Enlarge the star template on page 141. Trace it onto template plastic, including the center line, and cut it out. Trace around the template on the paper side of fusible web, mark the center line, and cut it out roughly.

5 Match up each white strip with a print strip. Stitch each pair together along the long edge to make a 4½ inch (11.4 cm) square, for a total of 4 squares.

6 Press the fusible web stars to the back of the white/print squares, making sure the center line matches up with the seam line. Cut out the stars along the drawn lines.

7 Center the fabric stars in each pinwheel block, lining up the seam of each star with the seam of the pinwheel. Once you are happy with the placement, fuse the stars to the background, following the manufacturers' instructions. Stitch around the edge of each star to permanently attach them to the background.

> This block is really simple to make, and I've made it many times with many variations. I've used stars, circles, diamonds, and even holly leaves for Christmas bees. Enlarge or reduce the size of the shapes, and play around with the fabric placement to alter the effect of the block.
>
> — *Brioni*

⭐ flickering stars pillow

by John Q. Adams ■ finished size: 50 x 20 inches (127 x 50.8 cm)

Quilted pillow covers are always a great project idea when you want to try a new technique, display your favorite fabrics (or your new skills with stars!), or scratch that creative itch and make something quickly.

materials

- ☐ ⅔ yard (.6 m) of white solid fabric
- ☐ Fabric scraps in assorted color prints for star centers, points, and borders
- ☐ 1 piece of muslin, 54 x 24 inches (137.2 x 61 cm)
- ☐ 1 piece of batting, 54 x 24 inches (137.2 x 61 cm)
- ☐ 1 pillow form, 20 x 50 inches (50.8 x127 cm)
- ☐ 2 pieces of fabric for back panels, ⅔ yard (.6 m) each; these can be from the same fabric or from two complementary fabrics

note: *Charm packs would work well for both the solid and prints here!*

cutting

1 From white solid fabric, cut:
- □ 32 squares measuring 4½ inches (11.4cm)
- □ 24 squares measuring 2½ inches (6.4 cm)
- □ 2 rectangles measuring 1½ x 12½ inches (3.8 x 31.8 cm)

2 From assorted print fabrics, cut:
- □ 12 squares measuring 4½ inches (11.4 cm)
- □ 26 squares measuring 2½ inches (6.4 cm)
- □ 20 rectangles measuring 2½ x 5½ inches (6.4 x 14 cm)

3 From the backing fabric, cut:
- □ 1 piece measuring 20½ x 39 inches (52.1 x 99.1 cm)
- □ 1 piece measuring 20½ x 29 inches (52.1 x 73.7 cm)

assembly

4 To make the points of each star:
- □ From the 12 assorted 4½-inch (11.4 cm) squares, set aside four to be the star centers. Cut each of the remaining squares in half on the diagonal to create 24 triangles.
- □ Lay one triangle atop a 4½-inch (11.4 cm) white square with right sides together. The exact placement is not important, as varying the placement will give the stars their "twinkling" effect. Make sure the triangle extends past the edges of the square, and that the seam line will be more than ¼-inch (6 mm) from the corners.
- □ Stitch the pieces together with a ¼-inch (6 mm) seam on the long edge of the triangle **(FIGURE 14)**. Trim away excess fabric from the seam.
- □ Press open and trim to 4½ inches (11.4 cm) square.
- □ Repeat with another colored triangle on the opposite corner **(FIGURE 15)**.
- □ Repeat to make four blocks per star.

5 To assemble each star, arrange the following pieces in rows and stitch **(FIGURE 16)**. Trim each finished block to 12½ inches (31.8 cm).
- □ 4 pieced star points
- □ 4 white 4½-inch (11.4 cm) squares
- □ one 4½-inch (11.4 cm) center square

note: *Chain-piecing is a real time-saver here!*

6 Stitch the four star blocks together **(FIGURE 17)**, and stitch the white 1½ x 12½-inch (3.8 x 31.8 cm) rectangles to each end.

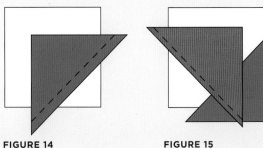

FIGURE 14   FIGURE 15

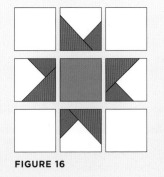

FIGURE 16

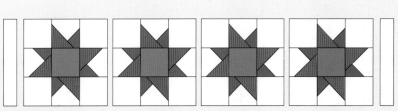

FIGURE 17

7 To complete the patchwork **(FIGURE 18)**:

- ☐ Join together the 2½-inch (31.8 cm) squares to make two strips. Use 13 print squares and 12 white squares for each strip. Start and end with a print and alternate between print and white. The finished strips will measure 2½ x 50½ inches (6.4 x 128.3 cm).
- ☐ Stitch these strips to the top and the bottom of the row of stars.
- ☐ Join together the remaining 20 print rectangles in two strips of 10, end-to-end along their short sides. The finished strips will measure 2½ x 51 inches (6.4 x 129.5 cm).
- ☐ Stitch these strips to the top and the bottom of the piecework.

8 Make a quilt sandwich with the pillow top centered on top of the slightly larger batting and muslin. Quilt as desired, through all three layers. The example was quilted with an all-over meandering stipple pattern.

9 Prepare the envelope back:

- ☐ Fold the smaller piece of backing fabric in half, lengthwise, to make a 20½ x 14½-inch (52.1 x 36.8 cm) rectangle. Press well to create a crisp folded end.
- ☐ For the remaining backing piece, make a ¼-inch (6 mm) double-fold hem on one short side. This will result in a 20½ x 38½-inch (52.1 x 97.8 cm) panel.

optional: *You can add binding to the folded edge for a more finished look. In the example, the designer made a 2½ x 20½-inch (6.4 x 52.1 cm) double-fold binding strip from scrap print fabric and stitched it to the folded edge of the smaller backing piece. This strip is then visible on the back of the finished pillow.*

10 To assemble the pillow:

- ☐ Lay out the pillow top with the right side facing up.
- ☐ Lay the smaller backing piece on top with its short raw edge aligned with the left side of the pillow top.
- ☐ Lay the larger backing piece on top of both layers with its short raw edge aligned with the right side of the pillow top. There will be approximately 5 inches (12.7 cm) of overlap between the two backing pieces. Pin well around all four sides.
- ☐ Stitch around all four sides using a ¼-inch (6 mm) seam allowance, pivoting at the corners. You might want to go around twice for added strength and seam reinforcement. Backstitch at the start and end of your seam.
- ☐ Trim the corners without cutting into your seam. Turn the pillow cover right side out and gently push out the corners.
- ☐ Insert the pillow form, and you're finished.

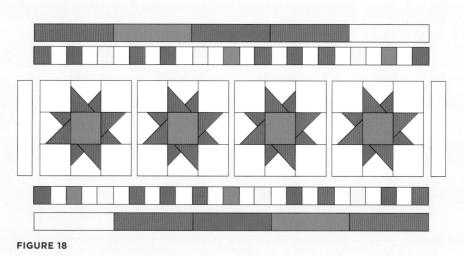

FIGURE 18

★ nordic star quilt

by Tacha Bruecher ■ *finished size:* 60 x 84 inches (152.4 x 213.4 cm)

Inspiration for this quilt came from Nordic style sweaters, which often combines one or two focal strips of pattern with negative space. There are actually three types of stars in this quilt: the center stars (which are similar to Dresden Plate blocks, page 96) and the two border stars.

materials

- ☐ Template plastic
- ☐ Templates (page 141)
- ☐ 5 fat quarters of different purple prints (large blades and some border stars)
- ☐ ½ yard (.5 m) of medium blue print fabric (small blades)
- ☐ 1 yard (.9 m) of light brown linen (background and border stars)
- ☐ ½ yard (.5 m) of gray print fabric, or 2 fat quarters and a 10-inch (25.4 cm) square of different gray prints (star's center and border stars)
- ☐ Freezer paper
- ☐ 4½ yards (4.1 m) of white solid fabric
- ☐ ½ yard (.5 m) of charcoal solid fabric, or 2 yards (1.8 m) if you want continuous strips
- ☐ 1 fat quarter of a plum print, or 2 fat eighths of different plum prints
- ☐ 1 fat eighth of a dark blue print
- ☐ 2 fat quarters of different aqua prints
- ☐ 1 piece of batting, 68 x 92 inches (172.7 x 233.7 cm)
- ☐ 5 yards (4.6 m) of backing fabric
- ☐ Binding fabric: 8 strips measuring 2½ inches (6.4cm) x the width of the fabric

To simplify the construction of this quilt, the instructions are organized in sections:

- □ *Primary Star Blocks*
- □ *Primary Star Strip, with the pieced squares above and below it*
- □ *Border Star Strips, with A blocks and B blocks, at the top and bottom of the quilt*
- □ *Final Assembly, of all the pieces*

Cut the pieces for each section as you come to it, rather than cutting everything at once. This will make it much easier to keep track of your pieces.

Primary Star Blocks

cutting

1 Enlarge the templates on page 141. Trace them onto template plastic, cut them out, and label them A, B, and C accordingly.

2 From the purple fat quarters, cut eight of template A from each of the five prints (for a total of 40 pieces). Set aside leftover fabric for border stars.

3 From the medium blue print, cut 40 template B pieces.

4 From the gray print(s), cut five squares measuring 3 inches (7.6 cm). Set aside leftover fabric for border stars.

5 From the linen fabric, cut five squares measuring 10½ inches (26.7 cm) for the background. Set aside leftover fabric for border stars.

assembly

6 Make the blades for each block:
- ☐ Select one set of eight purple A template pieces and eight blue B template pieces.
- ☐ Fold each A and B piece in half lengthways, right sides facing, and stitch along the top **(FIGURE 19)**.
- ☐ Turn the blade right side out and push out the point with a point turner (such as a chopstick). Fold the stitched fabric to the back of the blade, center the seam, and press it flat.

7 To make each star:
- ☐ Stitch a B piece to the right of each A piece **(FIGURE 20)**. Stitch to the end of each A piece even though the B piece does not reach that far. The stitching will help you turn under the right amount when appliquéing the star to the background square.
- ☐ Stitch the pairs together into a star shape and press well, turning the seam allowance under on the top parts of the A shape.

8 Center each star on a linen square and pin. Machine-stitch each blade in place, starting from the inside circle **(FIGURE 21)**. If you do not want your stitches to show, hand-sew the appliqué instead.

9 Make the centers:
- ☐ Trace around template C onto freezer paper five times. Cut out the circle shapes and fuse them to the wrong side of the five gray squares. Press the seam allowances to the back.
- ☐ Center each circle on a star and pin. Hand-sew in place, and when about 1 inch (2.5 cm) from the end, use a pin to pull the freezer paper out. Finish sewing in place.

10 Finish making all five blocks, and trim each one to 10½ inches (26.7 cm) square.

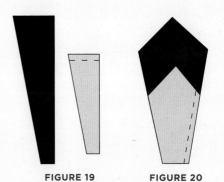

FIGURE 19   FIGURE 20

FIGURE 21

Primary Star Strip

cutting

1 From white solid fabric, cut the following pieces, then set aside the remaining fabric for border stars:

☐ 1 rectangle measuring 35½ x 60½ inches (90.2 x 153.7 cm), set aside for Final Assembly

☐ 6 strips measuring 1 x 60½ inches (2.5 x 153.7 cm)

☐ 4 strips measuring 1½ x 60½ inches (3.8 x 153.7 cm), set aside for the Border Star strips

☐ 1 rectangle measuring 12½ x 60½ inches (31.8 x 153.7 cm), set aside for Final Assembly

☐ 8 strips measuring 1¼ x 10½ inches (3.2 x 26.7 cm)

☐ 2 strips measuring 1½ x 10½ inches (3.8 x 26.7 cm)

☐ 6 strips measuring 1½ x 12 inches (3.8 x 30.5 cm)

☐ 4 strips measuring 1½ x 12¼ inches (3.8 x 31.1 cm)

☐ 54 strips measuring 1½ x 5½ inches (3.8 x 14 cm)

☐ 6 squares measuring 1½ inches (3.8 cm)

☐ 6 strips measuring 1½ x 4½ inches (3.8 x 11.4 cm)

2 From charcoal solid fabric, cut:

☐ 4 strips measuring 1 x 12½ inches (2.5 x 31.8 cm)

☐ 4 strips measuring 1 x 60½ inches (2.5 x 153.7 cm), set two aside for Final Assembly

3 From each of the plum, dark blue, and aqua prints, cut 20 squares measuring 1½ inches (3.8 cm), for a total of 60 squares. Set aside leftover fabric for border stars.

- -

assembly

4 Add border strips to the primary stars (**FIGURE 22**):

☐ Arrange the primary star blocks in a row of five. Stitch the eight white 1¼ x 10½-inch (3.2 x 26.7 cm) strips to the sides of each block except for the out-side edges on the end blocks. To those edges, stitch the two white 1½ x 10½-inch (3.8 x 26.7 cm) strips.

☐ Stitch the six white 1½ x 12-inch (3.8 x 15.25 cm) strips to the top and bottom edges of the three center blocks. Stitch the four white 1½ x 12¼-inch (3.8 x 31.1 cm) strips to top and bottom edges of the outside blocks.

☐ Stitch the blocks into a row with a 12½-inch (31.8 cm) charcoal strip between each block.

☐ Stitch long charcoal strips to the top and bottom of the star row. Set the remaining charcoal strips aside for Final Assembly.

5 Make the six pieced-square strips:

☐ For each strip, gather 10 of the 1½-inch (3.8 cm) squares (all of 1 color) and 9 of the white 1½ x 5½-inch (3.8 x 14 cm) strips.

☐ Stitch them into one long strip, alternating squares and rectangles, starting and ending with a color squares.

☐ To achieve the staggered rows, stitch a white 1½-inch (3.8 cm) square to one end of each strip, and stitch a white 1½ x 4½-inch (3.8 x 11.4 cm) strip to the other end.

6 Using the photograph as a guide, arrange the strips as follows:

☐ One plum square strip, one aqua square strip (rotated in the opposite direction), and one dark blue square strip, with one white 1½ x 60½-inch (3.8 x 153.7 cm) strip below each one.

☐ The primary star strip

☐ One dark blue square strip, one aqua square strip (rotated in the opposite direction), and one plum square strip, with one white 1½ x 60½-inch (3.8 x 153.7 cm) strip above each one.

☐ Stitch these strips together.

FIGURE 22

Border Star Strips

cutting

1 For block A, cut the following pieces from leftover fabrics:

- □ plum prints, 12 sets of four matching 1-inch (2.5 cm) squares (total of 48 squares)
- □ white fabric, 12 squares measuring 1 inch (2.5 cm)
- □ linen fabric, 48 strips measuring 1 x 2¼ inches (2.5 x 5.7 cm)
- □ gray prints, 12 sets of four matching 2¾-inch (7 cm) squares (total of 48 squares)

2 For block B, cut the following pieces from leftover fabrics:

- □ purple fat quarters, 12 sets of four matching 1½-inch (3.8 cm) squares (total of 48 squares)
- □ gray print(s), 12 squares measuring 1½ inches (3.8 cm)
- □ aqua prints, 96 squares measuring 1½ inches (3.8 cm)
- □ white fabric, 48 squares measuring 2½ inches (3.8 cm)
- □ white fabric, 48 squares measuring 1½ inches (3.8 cm)

assembly

3 Assemble the pieces for each block A:

- □ 4 gray squares
- □ 4 plum squares
- □ 1 white square
- □ 4 linen strips

4 Make each block A **(FIGURE 23)**:

- □ Stitch a plum square to one end of a linen strip. Repeat to make four.
- □ Stitch two gray squares to opposite sides of a plum/linen strip. Repeat to make two.
- □ Stitch two pieced plum/linen strips to opposite sides of a white square.
- □ Assemble the block as shown and stitch the pieces together, taking care to line up the seams.
- □ Make 12 A blocks, each measuring 5½ inches (14 cm) square.

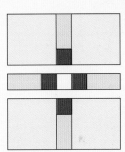

FIGURE 23

5 Assemble the piece for each block B:

- □ 4 white 2½-inch (6.4 cm) squares
- □ 4 white 1½-inch (3.8 cm) squares
- □ 4 matching purple print squares
- □ 1 gray square
- □ 8 aqua squares

6 Make the units for each block B:

- □ On the wrong side of all the aqua squares, draw a diagonal line from one corner to the opposite corner.
- □ Line up the aqua square with the corner of a white 2½-inch (6.4 cm) square **(FIGURE 24)**. Stitch along the diagonal line. Trim away the excess aqua fabric, open, and press.
- □ In the same way, stitch another aqua square to the opposite corner of the white square. Open and press.
- □ Stitch the remaining aqua squares to the remaining large white squares for a total of four aqua/white pieced squares.

- Stitch a small white square to each of the four purple squares.
- Stitch the purple edge of two of these strips to the gray square.

note: *Take care with directional prints. Lay out the block before sewing to make sure the orientation is correct.*

7 Assemble each block B **(FIGURE 25)** and stitch the rows together. Make 12 B-blocks, each measuring 5½ inches (14 cm) square.

8 Lay out the blocks in two rows of 12 blocks, alternating A and B blocks in each row. Stitch the rows together.

9 Stitch a 1½ x 60½-inch (3.8 x 153.7 cm) white strip (cut in step 1, page 86) to the top and bottom edges of both pieced rows.

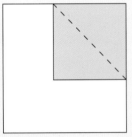

FIGURE 24

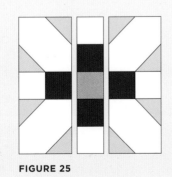

FIGURE 25

final assembly

1 Lay out the sections of the quilt as follows:
- 1 border star strip at the top
- 1 of the charcoal 1 x 60½-inch (2.5 x 153.7 cm) strips set aside earlier
- 12½ x 60½-inch (31.8 x 153.7 cm) rectangle set aside earlier
- Primary Star strip
- 35½ x 60½-inch (90.2 x 153.7 cm) rectangle set aside earlier
- remaining charcoal strip set aside earlier
- remaining border star strip

2 Stitch the rows together. Your quilt top is complete!

3 Refer to pages 135-137 for tips on basting, quilting and binding your quilt.

polygons

A POLY-WHAT?! The definition of a polygon is a many-sided flat shape with at least three straight sides (but typically five or more). We've included quirky shapes that don't seem to fit into a chapter of their own. Here they are: hexagons, pentagons, wedges, and other uncommon shapes that can add interest to your quilts.

The idea of piecing many different angles can be intimidating. To ease you into feeling more comfortable with polygons, we have included a variety of polygon blocks. Some are made from pure polygon shapes, and some are simpler shapes that together create a polygon shape.

Many true polygon shapes (for example the hexagon or pentagon) are popular in English paper piecing (see page 133). This method is an ideal way to learn how to work with polygons. English paper piecing is also a great on-the-go project that can be taken on car journeys (when you're a passenger) or even sewn up while sitting in the doctor's office. Some of the blocks and both of the quilts are made using this method. For more complicated and multi-faceted polygon sewing, try using different polygon shapes together to form a single larger shape.

Geometry was never this much fun! Join us for a refresher course on hexagons, pentagons, and other multi-sided shapes.

wedge wave

by KATY JONES

CUTTING

note: *In addition to fabric, you will also need template plastic.*

1 Enlarge the wedge template on page 142. Trace it onto template plastic and cut it out.

2 Trace around the template on the wrong side of 11 different blue solid fabric scraps. Cut out the shapes.

3 From background fabric, cut two rectangles measuring 5½ x 13 inches (14 x 33 cm).

- -

ASSEMBLY

4 Starting with a wedge that is narrow-end-up, arrange the wedges in a row, rotating the ends each time as seen in the block. Move the wedges around to find an arrangement that you like.

5 Stitch the wedges in order, right sides together, matching the corners as shown **(FIGURE 1)**. Press the finished strip. Draw a line down the center of the wedges at both ends and trim them to make a rectangular strip.

6 Stitch the background strips to the top and bottom edges of the center strip. Press and square up as needed.

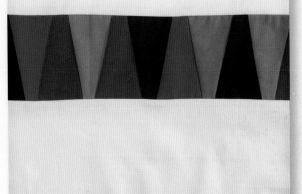

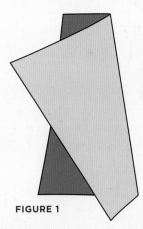

FIGURE 1

The basic tumbler or wedge shape is incredibly versatile. This exact same wedge shape is the basis of the Dresden Plate block on page 96, but it couldn't look more different when it's in this modern setting. —*Katy*

four flies

by JOHN Q. ADAMS

CUTTING

1 From light blue solid fabric, cut:
- ☐ 4 squares measuring 3 inches (7.6cm)
- ☐ 8 squares measuring 2½ inches (6.4 cm)

2 From both medium blue and dark blue solid fabrics, cut:
- ☐ 2 squares measuring 3 inches (7.6 cm)
- ☐ 4 squares measuring 2½ inches (6.4 cm)

3 From white solid fabric, cut:
- ☐ 2 squares measuring 3 inches (7.6 cm)
- ☐ 1 square measuring 2½ inches (6.4 cm)

4 From light gray solid fabric, cut:
- ☐ 6 squares measuring 3 inches (7.6 cm)
- ☐ 3 squares measuring 2½ inches (6.4 cm)

- -

ASSEMBLY

5 Make four half-square triangles (page 131), using two 3-inch (7.6 cm) light blue squares and the two 3-inch (7.6 cm) white squares. Trim each pieced square to 2½ inches (6.4 cm).

6 Assemble and stitch the Shoo Fly block as shown **(FIGURE 2)**, using:
- ☐ four 2½-inch (6.4 cm) light blue squares
- ☐ the 2½-inch (6.4 cm) white square **(FIGURE 2)**

7 Make 12 half-square triangles with the remaining 3-inch (7.6 cm) light gray squares and two 3-inch (7.6 cm) squares of each shade of blue.

8 Assemble and stitch three more Shoo Fly blocks.

9 Arrange the squares to match the block photo, and then stitch them together.

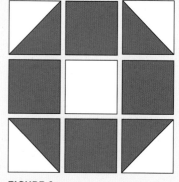

FIGURE 2

heart to heart
by BRIONI GREENBERG

CUTTING

1 From each of the black and white heart fabrics, cut:
- ☐ 4 squares measuring 2 inches (5.1 cm)
- ☐ 4 squares measuring 1½ inches (3.8 cm)

2 From each of two different background fabrics, cut:
- ☐ 2 squares measuring 2 inches (5.1cm)
- ☐ 2 squares measuring 1½ inches (3.8 cm)
- ☐ 4 strips measuring 1½ x 3½ inches (3.8 x 8.9 cm)
- ☐ 4 strips measuring 1½ x 5½ inches (3.8 x 14 cm)

3 From border fabric, cut:
- ☐ 2 strips measuring 1½ x 12½ inches (3.8 x 31.8 cm)
- ☐ 2 strips measuring 1½ x 10½ inches (3.8 x 26.7 cm)

ASSEMBLY

4 For the first heart unit, make two half-square triangles (page 131) using a 2-inch (5.1 cm) heart fabric square and a 2-inch (5.1 cm) background fabric square. Trim the pieced squares to 1½ inches (3.8 cm).

5 Using the diagram as a guide **(FIGURE 3)**, stitch together the following pieces (using matching colors) to form the heart unit.
- ☐ the two half-square triangles you just made
- ☐ one 1½-inch (3.8 cm) background square
- ☐ two 1½-inch (3.8 cm) heart fabric squares
- ☐ one 2-inch (5.1 cm) heart fabric square
- ☐ 2 background strips measuring 1½ x 3½ inches (3.8 x 8.9 cm)
- ☐ 2 background strips measuring 1½ x 5½ inches (3.8 x 14 cm)

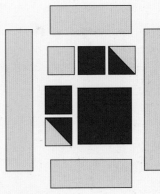

FIGURE 3

6 Complete three more heart units in the same way.

7 Arrange the four heart units so that the bottom of each heart points towards the center of the block. Join the units together.

8 Stitch the shorter border strips to each side of the block and press the seams. Stitch the remaining border strips to the top and bottom of the block, and press the seams.

tire tracks

by TACHA BRUECHER

CUTTING

note: *In addition to fabrics, you will also need template plastic.*

1 From different coordinating solid fabrics, cut 33 squares measuring 3 inches (7.6 cm).

2 From gray solid fabric, cut:
- ☐ 2 strips measuring 1 x 10½ inches (2.5 x 26.7 cm)
- ☐ 2 strips measuring 1½ x 10½ inches (3.8 x 26.7 cm)
- ☐ 2 strips measuring 1½ x 12½ inches (3.8 x 31.8 cm)

- -

ASSEMBLY

3 Enlarge the template on page 142. Trace it onto template plastic and cut it out.

4 Trace around the template on the wrong side of each of the 33 squares.

5 Cut out the shapes and arrange them in three strips of 11, with the pointed ended facing the center of each strip **(FIGURE 4)**.

6 Stitch the pieces together, starting and ending each Y-seam ¼-inch (.6 cm) from the edge. Draw a line down the center of the overhanging templates on the ends and trim each strip to 10½ inches (26.7 cm) in length.

7 Arrange the strips in three columns with the 1 x 10½-inch (2.5 x 26.7 cm) gray strips in between. Stitch the strips together, and press.

8 Stitch the shorter gray strips to the top and the bottom of the block. Stitch the remaining gray strips to the sides of the block.

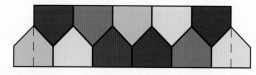

FIGURE 4

castle walls

by JOHN Q. ADAMS

CUTTING

1 From both dark gray and medium gray solid fabrics, cut four squares measuring 2½ inches (6.4 cm).

2 From navy blue solid fabric, cut four squares measuring 4½ inches (11.4 cm).

3 From white solid fabric, cut:
- ☐ 16 squares measuring 2½ inches (6.4 cm)
- ☐ 1 square measuring 4½ inches (11.4 cm)

- -

ASSEMBLY

4 To make the pointed navy units:
- ☐ Draw a diagonal line on the back of two white 2½-inch (6.4 cm) squares.
- ☐ Align a white square with the top right corner of a navy blue 4½-inch (11.4 cm) square. Stitch the squares together along the line.
- ☐ Trim the excess fabric ¼ inch (.6 cm) away from the sewn seam.
- ☐ Press open.
- ☐ Repeat with another white square on the top left corner of the block.

5 Repeat step 4 with the remaining three navy blue squares and six more white 2½-inch (6.4 cm) squares.

6 Assemble the full block according to the diagram **(FIGURE 5)**.

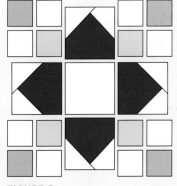

FIGURE 5

dresden plate

by KATY JONES

CUTTING

note: *In addition to fabrics, you will also need template plastic and a 5-inch (12.7 cm) square of freezer paper or cardstock.*

1 Draw a 4-inch (10.2 cm) diameter circle onto cardstock or freezer paper, then cut it out. Trace around the circle onto background fabric. Cut out the circle approximately ¼ inch (6 cm) larger than the template all the way round.

2 Also from background fabric, cut one square measuring 12½ inches (31.8 cm).

3 Enlarge the template on page 143. Trace it onto template plastic and cut it out.

4 Trace around the template on the wrong side of assorted blue fabrics 16 times, and cut out the shapes.

ASSEMBLY

5 To form each blade:
- ☐ Fold the template shape in half across the width, right sides together, and stitch along the top (wider) edge with a ¼-inch (6 mm) seam **(FIGURE 6)**.
- ☐ Turn the blade right side out and push out the point with a point turner. Fold the stitched fabric to the back of the blade, center the seam, and press it flat **(FIGURE 7)**.

6 Arrange the blades in a circle to your liking. Stitch the blades together along the long edges in sets of four, to form 4 quarters **(FIGURE 8)**. Stitch these quarters together to form a ring. Press all the seams to one side, taking care not to stretch the ring out of shape.

7 Fold the background square in half, then fold it in half again to form quarters. Gently press the folded square, then unfold it. Center the ring, right side up, in the center of the background square; line up the points of the top, bottom, and side blades with the fold lines. Pin well, then use a blind stitch or very small stitch to carefully hand-sew the ring to the background fabric.

8 Fold the circle into quarters and press gently. Open up the circle and realign it with the circle template. Carefully finger press the edges of the circle around the circle template to form a narrow hem. Remove the template and center the circle over the blades, matching the pressed quarter lines of the circle with the pressed quarter lines on the background fabric. Be sure to cover the raw edges of the ring beneath the circle. Pin well and hand-sew in place.

FIGURE 6   FIGURE 7

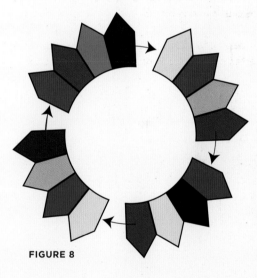

FIGURE 8

pentagon flower
by BRIONI GREENBERG

CUTTING

1 From background fabric, cut a 12½-inch (31.8 cm) square.

2 From assorted fabrics, cut out 3 inches (7.6 cm) squares as follows:
- ☐ 1 for the hexagon center
- ☐ 6 for the inner row of pentagons
- ☐ 12 for the outer row of pentagons

- -

ASSEMBLY

3 Enlarge the hexagon and pentagon templates on page 142. Cut out one hexagon and 16 pentagon pieces.

4 Using the English paper piecing method (page 133), pin the hexagon and pentagon papers to the fabric squares, fold over the fabric edges, and baste.

5 Using the photo as a guide, sew all the pieces together to form the flower. Remove the basting stitches and remove the paper shapes.

6 Fold the background fabric in half and then in half again. Gently press along the folds, then open up the square and lay it flat. Center the flower on the background with top and side seams aligned with the pressed lines. Pin in place.

7 Machine-stitch around the edge of the strip to attach the flower to the background.

bathroom tile

by TACHA BRUECHER

CUTTING

1 From assorted fabrics, cut out the following pieces:

- □ dark blue solid, 8 rectangles measuring 2½ x 5 inches (6.4 x 12.7cm)
- □ medium blue solid, 4 rectangles measuring 2½ x 5 inches (6.4 x 12.7 cm)
- □ light blue solid, 4 squares measuring 2½ inches (6.4 cm)
- □ light gray solid, 1 square measuring 2½ inches (6.4 cm)
- □ medium gray solid, 1 square measuring 12½ inches (31.8 cm)

2 Enlarge the hexagon template on page 142. Trace it onto printer paper to make 12 paper templates. Also draw and cut out five paper templates measuring 2 inches (5.1 cm) square.

ASSEMBLY

3 Using the English paper piecing method (page 133), pin the dark and medium blue rectangles to the 12 hexagon templates, fold over the fabric edges, and baste.

4 Baste the light gray and light blue squares to the five square templates.

5 Hand-sew the four medium blue hexagons in a ring around the light gray square **(FIGURE 9)**.

6 Hand-sew the eight dark blue hexagons in pairs and sew them to the medium blue ring you made in the previous step **(FIGURE 10)**.

7 Hand-sew the light blue squares between the dark blue hexagons **(FIGURE 11)**.

8 Press the block well and remove the paper templates. Center the block on the 12½-inch (31.8 cm) background square and pin carefully, making sure the seam allowance is folded under. Machine-stitch in place.

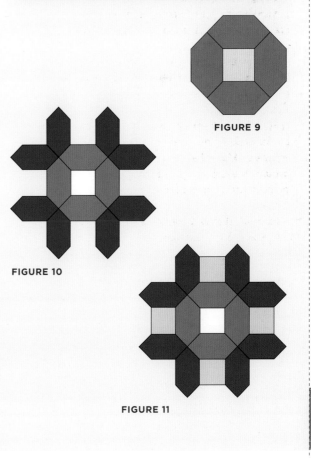

FIGURE 9

FIGURE 10

FIGURE 11

hexagon stripe

by BRIONI GREENBERG

CUTTING

1 From different background fabrics, cut four strips measuring 12½ x 3½ inches (31.8 x 8.9 cm).

2 From each of four different solid fabrics, cut six squares measuring 2½ inches (6.4 cm) for the hexagons.

3 Enlarge the hexagon template on page 142 20 times. Cut out 20 hexagons.

- -

ASSEMBLY

4 Stitch the four background strips together to make a 12½-inch (31.8 cm) square.

5 Using the English paper piecing method (page 133), pin the hexagon papers to the 2½-inch (6.4 cm) squares, fold over the fabric edges, and baste.

6 Stitch each set of hexagons (five of each color) together to form a strip, then press. Remove the basting stitches and remove the paper.

7 Place the strips on the background blocks and pin firmly in place. Machine-stitch around the edge of each strip to attach it to the background.

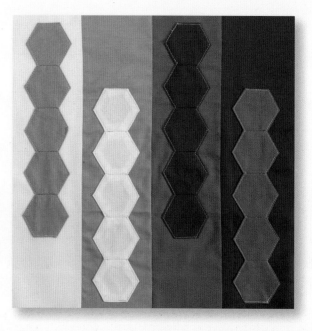

Little hexagons make me happy. Hexagons are traditionally used to make flowers, but I wanted to use them in a different way. I think the result is a really modern looking block, and I love how the value of the solid fabrics make the strips advance or recede.

— Brioni

windmill

by KATY JONES

CUTTING

1 From background fabric, cut one square measuring 7 inches (17.8 cm). Cut the square in half diagonally twice to make four triangles. These become the A pieces.

2 From the main blue fabric, cut 4 rectangles measuring 4½ x 8½ inches (11.4 x 21.6 cm). These are the B pieces.

- -

ASSEMBLY

3 Use a quilting ruler to mark a line at a 45° angle on one end of each B rectangle. Alternatively, mark a point 6 inches (15.2 cm) in from the top left hand side of the rectangle, and cut from the marked point to the opposite (bottom right hand) corner. The angle will be 45° **(FIGURE 12)**. Cut along this line and discard the small corner piece.

4 Stitch an A triangle to each B rectangle to form a larger triangle **(FIGURE 13)**.

5 Stitch the 4 triangles together. Press the seams open.

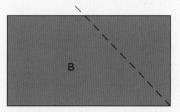

FIGURE 12

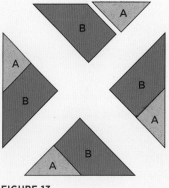

FIGURE 13

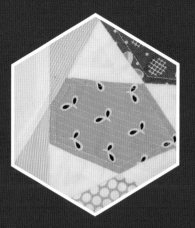

tickety tock clock

by Tacha Bruecher ■ finished size: approximately 16 x 18½ inches (40.6 x 47 cm)

Don't be afraid of polygons! This clock looks difficult, but once you have basted all the shapes to paper, it sews up pretty quickly. Fussy cut favorite motifs to give your clock a unique look. Or try using different fonts for the numbers or even leave the numbers off altogether.

materials

- ☐ 3 coordinating print fabrics, at least 10 inches (25.4 cm) square, for the primary color units
- ☐ 1 fat quarter of white solid fabric
- ☐ 1 fat eighth of a light gray solid fabric
- ☐ 1 additional print fabric scrap (for the 6 corners), 10 inches (25.4 cm) square
- ☐ Templates (page 142)
- ☐ 8-inch (20.3 cm) fussy-cut square for the center of clock; motif size is 3½ inches (8.9 cm) square
- ☐ Scraps of freezer paper
- ☐ 20-inch (50.8cm) square of stiff fusible interfacing
- ☐ Numerical stamps and fabric ink
- ☐ ½ yard (.5 m) of backing fabric
- ☐ Clock mechanism
- ☐ ¼ yard (.3 m) of binding fabric

cutting

1 From each of the three print fabrics, cut:
- ☐ 4 pieces measuring 3½ x 4½ inches (8.9 x 11. 4 cm)

2 From the white solid fabric, cut:
- ☐ 12 pieces measuring 2 x 3¼ inches (5.1 x 8.3 cm)
- ☐ 12 pieces measuring 2¼ x 2½ inches (5.7 x 6.4 cm)
- ☐ 12 pieces measuring 1¾ x 4½ inches (4.4 x 11.4 cm)

3 From the light gray solid, cut 12 pieces measuring 1¾ x 4¼ inches (4.4 x 10.8 cm).

4 From the additional print fabric scraps, cut:
- ☐ 6 pieces measuring 1¾ x 2¾ inches (4.4 x 2.75 cm)
- ☐ 1 strip measuring 2 x 4 inches (5.1 x 10.2 cm), for a hanging loop

5 Enlarge the shape templates on page 142. Cut out 12 each of the A, B, C, D, and E templates. Cut out six of the F template.

assembly

6 To assemble the inner ring of the clock, do the following:
- ☐ Pin the 12 A templates to the 12 larger print pieces, fold over the fabric edges, and baste. Trim the seam allowances roughly to the shape of the template to remove excess fabric from your seams.
- ☐ Pin the 12 B templates to the white 2 x 3¼-inch (5.1 x 8.3 cm) pieces and baste.
- ☐ Pin the 12 C templates to the white 2¼ x 2½-inch (5.7 x 6.4 cm) pieces and baste.
- ☐ Stitch a white B piece and a white C piece to the right hand side of each A piece **(FIGURE 14)**. Repeat with the remaining A, B, and C pieces.
- ☐ Arrange the stitched pieces in a circle, alternating the colors **(FIGURE 15)**. Stitch together.

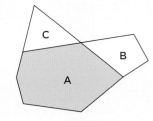

FIGURE 14

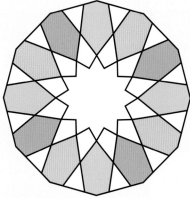

FIGURE 15

7 To attach the border:

- ☐ Pin the 12 D templates to the gray pieces and baste. Stitch these pieces around the circle, centered on the white C piece and extending half way across two A pieces **(FIGURE 16)**.
- ☐ Pin and baste six E templates to six of the remaining white pieces. Flip the remaining six E templates over and baste to the remaining white pieces. Arrange and sew these pieces around the circle **(FIGURE 17)**.
- ☐ Pin the six F templates to the remaining print pieces and baste. Stitch these pieces to the clock face in the gaps between the E pieces **(FIGURE 18)**.

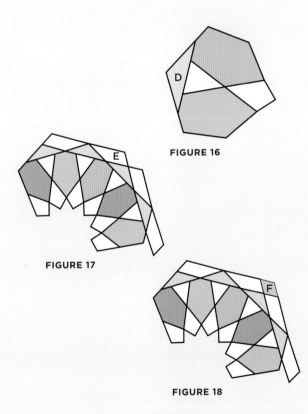

FIGURE 16

FIGURE 17

FIGURE 18

8 Position the 8-inch (20.3 cm) fussy-cut square behind the clock face so it shows through the central opening. Remove the paper templates from the clock parts that overlap the square and pin carefully, making sure both pieces lie flat. Hand-sew in place.

9 Use the numeral stamps and fabric ink to apply the numbers, following the manufacturer's instructions, to the clock face.

10 Remove all the paper templates except for the ones on the outside edges. Place the clock face right side up on the interfacing and fuse only the center of the clock face to the interfacing, following the manufacturer's instructions. Trim the interfacing to ¼ inch (6 mm) larger than the clock front on all sides. Remove the remaining paper templates from the clock front and fuse the unfused parts of the clock face to the interfacing. Trim any parts of the clock face that overhang the interfacing.

11 Make a hanging loop in the same way as double-fold binding:

- ☐ Fold the 2 x 4-inch (5.1 x 10.2 cm) strip in half lengthways, wrong sides facing, and press.
- ☐ Open up the strip and fold the edges into the center, and press again.
- ☐ Refold in half and stitch along both long edges.
- ☐ Fold in half widthwise to make the loop.

12 Cut the backing fabric into two pieces measuring 10 x 18 inches (25.4 x 45.7 cm) and 14 x 18 inches (35.6 x 45.7 cm). Place them right sides facing and insert the loop in the center, between the pieces. Sew together along the long edge and press.

13 Lay the backing wrong side up on a flat surface. Position the clock front on the backing making sure the seam on the backing piece runs from the 3 to 9 on the clock front.

note: *Make sure it is straight or the clock will hang at an angle.*

14 Refer to pages 135-137 for tips on basting and quilting.

15 Cut the binding fabric into strips that measure 2½ inches (6.4 cm) x width of fabric, and bind the clock.

16 Mark the center of the clock face and use a craft knife to cut a very small hole. Insert the clock works through the hole and fix the clock hands in place following the manufacturer's instructions.

saw blade quilt

by Brioni Greenberg finished size: 78 x 92 inches (198.1 x 233.7 cm)
quilted by Christine at Father's Heart Quilting

No doubt you have some treasured fabric stashed away just waiting for that perfect project? This Saw Blade design is an ideal pattern to showcase special materials. There are endless possibilities and fabric choices, but whatever you choose to use is sure to create a dramatic effect!

materials

- ☐ Clear template plastic
- ☐ Templates (page 141)
- ☐ ½ yard (.5 m) of fabric A for the center of the saw blades (see Fabric Notes)
- ☐ 1¼ yard (1.1 m) of fabric B (innermost ring)
- ☐ 1¾ yards (1.6 m) of fabric C (middle ring)
- ☐ 2 yards (1.8 m) of fabric D (outer ring)
- ☐ 4½ yards (4.1 m) of background solid fabric
- ☐ Printer paper
- ☐ ¾ yards (.7 m) of binding fabric
- ☐ 5½ yards (5 m) of backing fabric
- ☐ Piece of batting, 86 x 98 inches (218.4 x 248.9 cm)
- ☐ Glue stick

fabric notes

The fabric requirements for fabric A assume that the centers of the saw blades are not fussy cut. If you wish to fussy cut the centers, the amount of fabric you need will depend on the size of the motif and the number of motifs to a repeat. You will need 20 motifs.

To change the look of the quilt, you can make all the blocks the same or use different color combinations. Depending on your color choices, you will need to adjust your fabric requirements and cutting list accordingly.

cutting

1 Enlarge the templates on page 141. Cut out 20 copies of template A and put them aside for now.

2 Trace the remaining templates onto clear template plastic and cut them out. (The clear plastic helps you see the design when you cut the pieces). Label each template with its number, and mark the top and bottom to help when constructing the blades.

note: *If you are fussy cutting the pieces, it's a good idea to also mark the template with some distinguishing feature at the center point or the outline of the motif. This helps you to position the template on the fabric in exactly the same way every time.*

3 From fabric A, cut 20 squares measuring 4½ inches (11.4 cm). Set them aside with the template A paper pieces.

4 Use templates B, C, and D to cut the following pieces.
- ☐ From fabric B, 320 of template B
- ☐ From fabric C, 320 of template C
- ☐ From fabric D, 320 of template D

5 From the background solid, cut:
- ☐ 100 of template E
- ☐ 100 of template F
- ☐ 100 of template G
- ☐ 100 of template H
- ☐ 4 strips measuring 5 x 92 inches (12.7 x 233.7 cm) for the border

6 From binding fabric, cut nine strips measuring 2½ inches (6.4 cm) x the width of the fabric.

assembly

6 You will make 20 of these blocks, and for each block you will need the following pieces. Organize the pieces into 20 piles containing:
- ☐ 1 octagon center (to be made later from template A)
- ☐ 16 of template B pieces
- ☐ 16 of template C pieces
- ☐ 16 of template D pieces
- ☐ 4 of template E pieces
- ☐ 4 of template F pieces
- ☐ 4 of template G pieces
- ☐ 4 of template H pieces

7 This block is made from 16 wedges. To make each wedge, stitch together one B, one C, and one D piece **(FIGURE 19)**. Repeat to make all 16 wedges.

8 To add the background pieces:
- ☐ Stitch a template E piece to the top of four of the wedges.
- ☐ Stitch a template F piece to the top of four of the wedges.
- ☐ Stitch a template G piece to the top of four of the wedges.
- ☐ Stitch a template H piece to the top of four of the wedges.
- ☐ Press all seams towards the outside of the wedge.

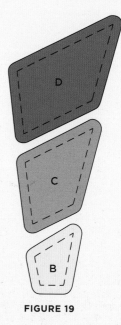

FIGURE 19

9 Stitch all the wedges together **(FIGURE 20)**.

10 Repeat steps 6, 7, 8, and 9 to make a total of 20 blocks.

11 To make the centers:
- ☐ Using the English paper piecing method (page 133), baste the fabric A squares to the paper A templates.
- ☐ Press each piece so the folds are nice and crisp. Clip the basting stitches and carefully remove the papers.
- ☐ Place an octagon in the middle of each block, making sure the bottoms of all the wedges are under the octagon. Pin carefully. Machine-stitch or hand-sew the appliqué in place.
- ☐ Trim the block to 17 inches (43.2 cm) square.

12 Arrange the blocks into five rows of four blocks. Stitch them together, making sure the seams between the blocks match up as closely as possible.

13 To add the border:
- ☐ Stitch a 5-inch (12.7 cm) border strip to both side edges of the quilt top.
- ☐ Stitch a 5-inch (12.7 cm) border strip to the top and bottom edges of the quilt top.

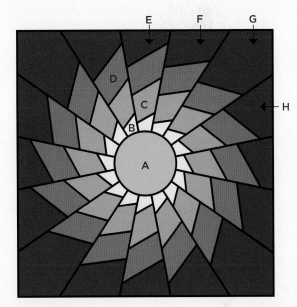

FIGURE 20

14 Refer to pages 135-137 for tips on basting, quilting, and binding your quilt.

diamonds

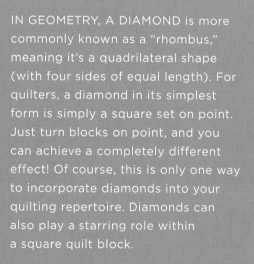

IN GEOMETRY, A DIAMOND is more commonly known as a "rhombus," meaning it's a quadrilateral shape (with four sides of equal length). For quilters, a diamond in its simplest form is simply a square set on point. Just turn blocks on point, and you can achieve a completely different effect! Of course, this is only one way to incorporate diamonds into your quilting repertoire. Diamonds can also play a starring role within a square quilt block.

Additionally, diamonds can be stretched in all different ways to make them as tall and thin or as short and squat as you like. And diamonds can be thought of as parallelograms—with opposite sides that are parallel to one another.

In this section, we've pulled together several ideas for quilt blocks and projects that feature diamond shapes and patterns for quilters of all skill levels. Have fun, be inspired, and challenge yourself—tilt your head and consider diamonds instead of squares for your next quilting project!

It's said that diamonds are a girl's best friend, but we much prefer ours in quilt form (especially John).

four eyes

by TACHA BRUECHER

CUTTING

1 From each of two gray prints and two orange prints, cut eight squares measuring 1½ inches (3.8 cm), for a total of 36 squares.

2 From both a blue print and an orange print, cut:
- ☐ 2 squares measuring 1½ inches (3.8 cm), for "eye" centers
- ☐ 4 strips measuring 1 x 5½ inches (2.5 x 14 cm) for borders
- ☐ 4 strips measuring 1 x 6½ inches (2.5 x 16.5 cm) for borders

3 From white solid fabric, cut:
- ☐ 16 strips measuring 1½ x 2½ inches (3.8 x 6.4 cm)
- ☐ 16 strips measuring 1½ x 2 inches (3.8 x 5.1 cm)
- ☐ 8 squares measuring 1½ inches (3.8 cm)

- -

ASSEMBLY

4 Assemble and stitch four "eye" units as follows **(FIGURE 1)**:
- ☐ Top row: two longer white strips and one colored square from step 1
- ☐ Second row: two shorter white strips and two matching color squares
- ☐ Third row: two white squares, two matching color squares, and one contrasting center square
- ☐ Fourth row: same as second row
- ☐ Fifth row: same as top row

5 Stitch the shorter contrasting borders to the sides of each block, then stitch the two longer contrasting borders to the top and bottom edges.

6 Use the photograph as a guide for arranging the diamond units into a four-patch block. Stitch them together in rows.

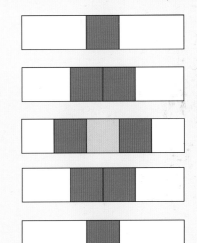

FIGURE 1

courtyard garden
by JOHN Q. ADAMS

CUTTING

1 From each of four different prints, cut a square measuring 4½ inches (11.4 cm).

2 From orange solid fabric, cut four squares measuring 2 inches (5.1 cm).

3 From gray solid (background) fabric, cut:
- ☐ 8 strips measuring 1½ x 4½ inches (3.8 x 11.4 cm)
- ☐ 8 strips measuring 1½ x 6½ inches (3.8 x 16.5 cm)
- ☐ 4 squares measuring 2 inches (5.1 cm)

- -

ASSEMBLY

4 To make the print center of each quarter-block unit:
- ☐ Draw a line on the back of each gray square along the diagonal.
- ☐ Align a gray square with the bottom right corner of a print square, right sides facing, and stitch along the line **(FIGURE 2)**. Trim the excess fabric from the corner, ¼-inch (6 mm) away from the sewn seam. Press the corner.
- ☐ Repeat to make three more print centers. Take care when using directional prints to line up the gray square with the appropriate corner.

5 To add the borders:
- ☐ Stitch the shorter gray strip to both sides of each block.
- ☐ Stitch the remaining longer strips to the top and bottom of each block.

6 To make the orange center square:
- ☐ Draw a diagonal line on the back of each orange solid square.
- ☐ Align the orange solid square with the bottom right corner of your upper left block. Stitch along the line **(FIGURE 3)**.
- ☐ Trim the seam and press, as you did in step 4.
- ☐ Repeat for the remaining three blocks.

note: *The corner placement of the orange square depends on its final block placement. Arrange the units together before stitching and mark which corner needs the orange piece.*

7 Join all four quadrants of your block together, with the orange triangles meeting in the center to form a diamond shape. Stitch and press.

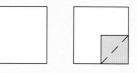

FIGURE 2

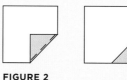

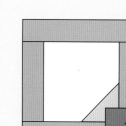

FIGURE 3

card trick

by KATY JONES

CUTTING

1 From each of a white solid, a blue print, and an orange print, cut:

- ☐ 2 squares measuring 5 inches (12.7 cm), then cut in half diagonally to make four triangles
- ☐ 1 square measuring 5¼ inches (13.3 cm), then cut in half diagonally twice to make four triangles

- -

ASSEMBLY

2 Refer to the construction diagram **(FIGURE 4)** for layout, and stitch the pieces together row by row. Be careful not to stretch the triangles out of shape; because they are cut on the bias, they are easier to distort than fabric cut along the grain.

3 Press seams open as you go, to reduce bulk where multiple points meet.

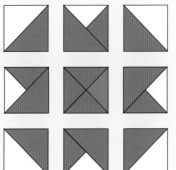

FIGURE 4

I love this traditional block; it's one of my all-time favorites! The illusion of the overlapping squares is most effective when you use highly contrasting colors or values in your fabric choices.
— *Katy*

diamond pinwheel

by BRIONI GREENBERG

CUTTING

ℕₒₜₑ: *In addition to fabrics, you will also need template plastic.*

1 From assorted fabrics, cut the following pieces:
- ☐ For the orange print background, 8 rectangles measuring 2¼ x 4¼ inches (5.7x 10.8 cm)
- ☐ For the blue diamonds, 4 rectangles measuring 3½ x 6½ inches (8.9 x 16.5 cm)
- ☐ From white solid fabric, 4 rectangles measuring 3½ x 6½ inches (8.9 x 16.5 cm)

2 Enlarge the diamond template on page 143. Trace the shape onto template plastic and cut it out.

3 Trace the template on the wrong side of the four diamond rectangles, then cut them out.

4 Cut four of the print background rectangles in half diagonally (from corner to corner) to make triangles. Cut the remaining four in the same way but in the opposite direction. For each diamond unit, you will need two triangles that have been cut in one direction and two that have been cut in the opposite direction.

ASSEMBLY

5 To make each diamond unit **(FIGURE 5)**:
- ☐ Stitch the background triangles at two diagonally opposite corners of a diamond shape. Press the seams away from the diamond.
- ☐ Stitch and press the remaining two triangles in the same way.
- ☐ Trim the unit to 3½ x 6½ inches (8.9 x 16.5 cm).
- ☐ Repeat for the remaining three diamond units.

6 Stitch each diamond unit to a white rectangle, along the long side, to make a square.

7 Assemble the squares, rotating the position of the diamond shapes to match the photograph. Stitch the four squares together.

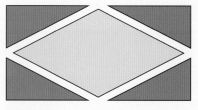

FIGURE 5

I really love how the blue centers recede. The block would also look great with all the diamonds pointing in the same direction.
— *Brioni*

diamond nine-patch

by JOHN Q. ADAMS

CUTTING

1 From assorted fabrics, cut the following pieces:
- orange print, 4 squares measuring 4½ inches (11.4 cm)
- blue print, 5 squares measuring 4½ inches (11.4 cm)
- orange solid, 4 squares measuring 2½ inches (6.4 cm)
- blue solids and prints, 16 squares measuring 2½ inches (6.4 cm)

- -

ASSEMBLY

2 To make each of the orange-diamond squares (for a total of four squares):
- Draw a diagonal line on the back of each of the 16 blue solid or print squares.
- Align a blue square on the bottom right corner of one of the orange print squares, and stitch along the line **(FIGURE 6)**. Trim the excess fabric ¼ inch (6 mm) away from the seam, and press the corner.
- Repeat for the other three corners of the square **(FIGURE 7)**.

3 Repeat step 2, using a blue print square in the center of the block and the four orange solid squares for the corners.

4 Use the block photo as a guide to assemble your final block. Stitch the blocks into rows, then stitch the rows together.

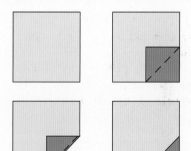

FIGURE 6

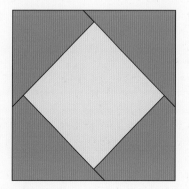

FIGURE 7

interlocked

by TACHA BRUECHER

CUTTING

1 From white solid fabric, cut:
- ☐ 1 strip measuring 1¾ x 3½ inches (4.4 x 8.9 cm), for cutting triangles
- ☐ 2 strips measuring 1⅜ x 6½ inches (3.5 x 16.5 cm)
- ☐ 2 strips measuring 1⅜ x 9½ inches (3.5 x 24.1 cm)
- ☐ 2 rectangles measuring 9 x 8 inches (22.9 x 20.3 cm), then cut in half diagonally

2 Cut the following pieces from 4 different orange print fabrics:
- ☐ 1 strip measuring 1⅜ x 3½ inches (3.5 x 8.9 cm), and 1 strip measuring 1⅜ x 8 inches (3.5 x 20.3 cm)
- ☐ 1 strip measuring 1⅜ x 4½ inches (3.5 x 11.4 cm), and 1 strip measuring 1⅜ x 9½ inches (3.5 x 24.1 cm)
- ☐ 1 strip measuring 1⅜ x 5½ inches (3.5 x 14 cm), and 1 strip measuring 1⅜ x 9½ inches (3.5 x 24.1 cm)
- ☐ 2 strips measuring 1⅜ x 10 inches (3.5 x 25.4 cm)

3 Cut the same pieces listed in step 2, this time from four different blue fabrics.

4 Use the markings on a transparent ruler to cut two white 60°-degree equilateral triangles from the first white strip. All 3 sides of the triangle will be 3½ inches (8.9 cm).

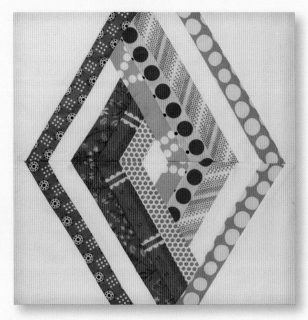

ASSEMBLY

5 The block is assembled and stitched in 2 mirrored halves. Here's how to make the triangle portion of the first half:
- ☐ Stitch the orange and white strips as shown **(FIGURE 8)** to one side of a white triangle, starting with the triangle and the shortest strip. Center the strip on the side of the triangle and stitch, then center the next strip and stitch, until all strips are stitched. Trim the ends in a direct line extending from the triangle.
- ☐ Stitch the blue strips as shown **(FIGURE 9)** to the opposite side of the triangle. Trim the ends and trim the triangle to a height of 6½ inches (16.5 cm).
- ☐ Stitch white and orange strips to the right side and a blue strip to the left side of the triangle as shown **(FIGURE 10)**. Trim the ends.

6 Stitch the mirror image of the triangle you just made, following the same steps, but with the opposite colors **(FIGURE 11)**.

7 Stitch the white half-rectangles to either side of your triangle blocks **(FIGURE 12)**. Open and press. Trim the bottom of your block to make a straight line.

8 Line up the seams of the two halves of your block. Pin each seam to make sure the strips line up properly. Stitch the halves together, open, press, and trim to 12½ inches (31.8 cm) square.

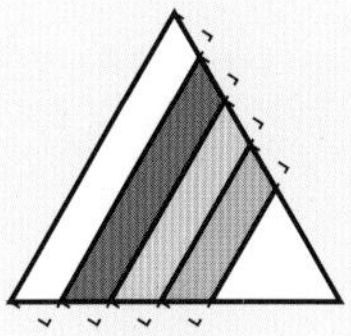

FIGURE 8

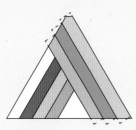

FIGURE 9

FIGURE 10

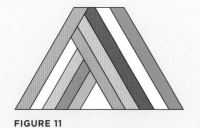

FIGURE 11

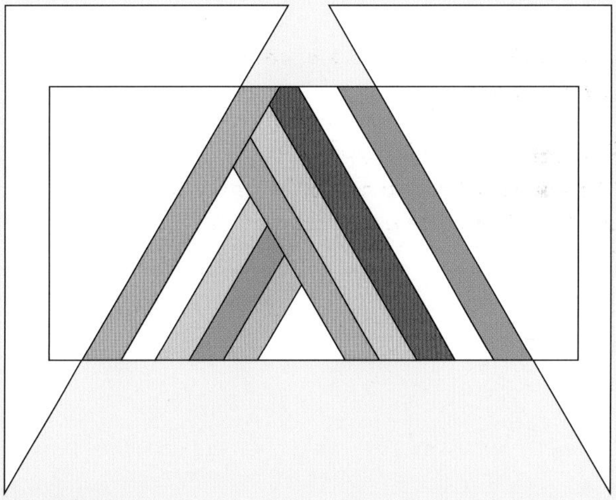

FIGURE 12

economy patch
by KATY JONES

CUTTING

1 From assorted fabrics, cut the following pieces:

- ☐ blue print, 1 square measuring 6½ inches (16.5cm)
- ☐ orange print, 1 square measuring 7¼ inches (18.4 cm), then cut in half diagonally twice to make four triangles
- ☐ white solid, 2 squares measuring 7 inches (17.8 cm), then cut into half diagonally to make four triangles

ASSEMBLY

2 To make the block **(FIGURE 13)**:

- ☐ Stitch orange triangles to both sides of the blue center square. Press seams out towards the triangles.
- ☐ Stitch orange triangles to the top and bottom of the center square. Press seams out towards the triangles again.
- ☐ Stitch a white triangle to each edge and press the seams out.

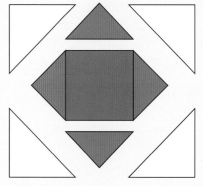

FIGURE 13

diamond in a diamond

by BRIONI GREENBERG

CUTTING

note: *In addition to fabrics, you will also need template plastic.*

1 Enlarge the templates on page 143. Trace each of the templates onto template plastic and cut the shapes out.

2 From white solid fabric, cut eight pieces using template A.

3 From each of eight different prints (four orange and four blue), cut one piece using template B. Flip the template over and cut another piece from each print.

- -

ASSEMBLY

4 Stitch matching print B triangles to both long sides of each of the white A triangles **(FIGURE 14)**, for a total of eight units.

5 Match up blue units with orange units and stitch them together on the longest edge to make four squares. The white triangles will make a diamond shape.

6 Arrange the four squares together to make a four-patch block with the blue prints turned to the inside and the points of the diamonds meeting in the middle. Stitch and press.

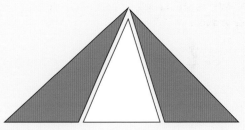

FIGURE 14

string diamond

by JOHN Q. ADAMS

CUTTING

note: *In addition to fabric, you will need four 6½-inch (16.5 cm) squares of scrap paper. The paper squares will be the foundation for each quadrant of the block (see page 134).*

1 From assorted blue and orange prints, cut strips of varying widths.

- -

ASSEMBLY

2 To start making the four quadrants of the block:
- ☐ Cut one of the print strips long enough to span from one corner of a paper foundation square to the opposite diagonal corner, including a slight overhang. Cut three more of the same length from the same fabric (one for each paper foundation).
- ☐ From a contrasting print, cut four more strips the same length as the first.
- ☐ Center one strip on the paper foundation and lay the contrasting strip on top, right sides together. Stitch through all three layers (two layers of fabric plus your paper foundation) along one edge of the strips, using a ¼-inch (6 mm) seam **(FIGURE 15)**.
- ☐ Press the piece open with the seam towards the second string.
- ☐ Repeat this step using the same fabric strips for the other three quadrants. The four blocks need to match to achieve the diamond effect.

tip: *Reduce the stitch length on your machine to make it easier to tear off the paper foundations.*

3 Continue sewing strips until you have completed half of each quadrant, then turn the block around and start working in the opposite direction.

4 Press each of the finished quadrants, then turn them over. Using the paper foundation as a guide, trim the block down to 6½-inch (41.9 cm) square. Carefully re-move the paper from the back of each block.

5 Assemble the block by rotating the quadrants until matching corners meet in the center. Stitch the quadrants together.

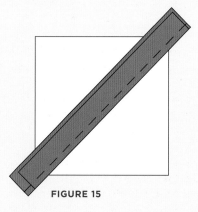

FIGURE 15

pinchers

by TACHA BRUECHER

CUTTING

1 Cut 2½ x 4-inch (6.4 x 10.2 cm) rectangles from each of the following fabrics:

- ☐ 3 from gray fabric
- ☐ 4 from blue print fabric
- ☐ 4 from a second blue print fabric
- ☐ 4 rectangles from orange print fabrics

2 From a light blue solid fabric, cut two strips measuring 1 x 12½ inches (2.5 x 31.8 cm).

3 From white solid fabric, cut:

- ☐ 2 strips measuring 2¼ x 12½ inches (5.7 x 31.8 cm)
- ☐ 1 strip measuring 8 x 12½ inches (20.3 x 31.8 cm)

4 Enlarge the diamond template on page 133. Trace it onto printer paper 15 times and cut out the shapes.

- -

ASSEMBLY

5 Baste the fabric rectangles to the diamond templates for English paper piecing (page 133), trimming the seam allowance as needed to reduce bulk.

6 Hand-sew four matching blue diamonds in pairs, then sew each pair to the sides of a gray diamonds **(FIGURE 16)**.

7 Sew together two more sets of diamonds to match the first, one with blue prints and one with orange prints. Sew the three units together and press well.

8 Remove the paper templates and carefully pin the pieced diamonds to the white 8 x 12½-inch (20.3 x 31.8 cm) strip. Make sure to tuck under the seam allowance. Machine-stitch in place about ⅛-inch (.3 cm) from the edge.

9 Add the sides of the block:

- ☐ Stitch the light blue strips to both sides of the center diamond strip.
- ☐ Stitch the remaining white strips to both sides of the diamond strip.
- ☐ Press and square up the block.

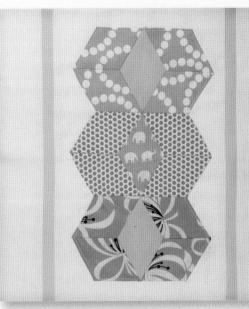

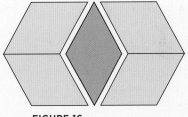

FIGURE 16

I used to spend summer holidays rock-pool fishing on the south coast of England. I was always a little wary of crabs pinching my toes! This block reminds me of a crab's pinchers.

— *Tacha*

starry hanging storage

by Brioni Greenberg ■ finished size: 14½ x 60 inches (36.8 x 152.4 cm)

Are you forever misplacing those crucial quilting notions? Or are you simply looking for a project that uses up all those itty bitty scraps that you just can't bear to throw away? This handy hanging organizer fits the bill.

materials

- ☐ 1¾ yards (1.6 m) of fabric for the background and backing
- ☐ Assorted brown scraps for pockets, approximately ¾ yard (.7 m) total
- ☐ Assorted red, orange, pink, and yellow small scraps for stars, approximately¾ yard (.7 m) total
- ☐ ½ yard (.5 m) of 96-inch-wide (243.8 cm) cotton batting
- ☐ 3 yards (2.7 m) of 20-inch-wide (50.8 cm) heavyweight fusible interfacing
- ☐ ½ yard (.5 m) of fabric for binding, or scrap 2½-inch (6.4 cm) strips
- ☐ Template (page 143)
- ☐ 6 inches (15.2 cm) of narrow twill tape to coordinate with the background
- ☐ Printer paper
- ☐ Glue stick

cutting

1 From background fabric, cut the following pieces:
- ☐ 2 rectangles measuring 14½ x 60 inches (36.8 x 152.4 cm)
- ☐ 3 rectangles measuring 13½ x 14½ inches (34.3 x 36.8 cm)
- ☐ 2 rectangles measuring 5½ x 14½ inches (14 x 36.8 cm)

2 From scraps (for pockets), cut:
- ☐ 48 rectangles measuring 3½ x 4 inches (8.9 x 10.2 cm)
- ☐ 8 rectangles measuring 4 x 4½ inches (10.2 x 11.4 cm)

3 From scraps (for stars), cut 174 pieces measuring 1½ x 2 inches (3.8 x 5.1 cm). If you want distinct stars-within-stars, cut 54 each of red, orange, and pink, and 12 of yellow for the small stars.

4 From batting, cut:
- ☐ 1 rectangle measuring 14½ x 60 inches (36.8 x 152.4 cm)
- ☐ 3 rectangles measuring 15½ x 16½ inches (39.4 x 41.9 cm)
- ☐ 2 rectangles measuring 7½ x 16½ inches (19 x 41.9 cm)

5 From heavyweight fusible interfacing, cut:
- ☐ 1 rectangle measuring 14½ x 60 inches (36.8 x 152.4 cm)
- ☐ 3 rectangles measuring 12½ x 14½ inches (31.8 x 36.8 cm)
- ☐ 2 rectangles measuring 4½ x 14½ inches (11.4 x 36.8 cm)

6 From binding fabric, cut four strips measuring 2½ inches (6.4 cm) x the width of the fabric.

assembly

7 Make the foundation/backing for the organizer:
- ☐ Collect the 14½ x 60-inch (36.8 x 152.4 cm) pieces of background/backing fabric, batting, and interfacing.
- ☐ Fuse the interfacing to the batting, following manufacturer's directions.
- ☐ Form a layer with the fused piece in between the two background/backing pieces. Pin the layers together.
- ☐ Stitch ⅛-inch (3 mm) all the way around the edges to hold the layers together.

8 Make the large pieced pocket fronts:
- ☐ Divide the 48 pocket rectangles into three piles of 16.
- ☐ Lay out each set of 16 rectangles into four rows of four, with the lengths placed horizontally. Stitch the pieces together in rows, then stitch the rows together.
- ☐ Trim the edges as needed to form three blocks measuring 12½ x 14½ inches (31.8 x 36.8 cm). Set aside.

9 Make the small pockets:
- ☐ Divide the remaining eight pocket rectangles into two piles.
- ☐ Arrange two rows of rectangles, with the lengths placed vertically.
- ☐ Stitch the rows together.

10 Enlarge the diamond template on page 143. Make five copies of the diamond paper templates and cut out 174 paper diamonds. (You will have some extras.) Using the English paper piecing method (page 133), baste all the star rectangles onto the templates.

tip: *Swipe each paper with a glue stick to make sure the papers stay in place while basting. The papers will still be really easy to remove when the quilt top is complete.*

11 You will need 54 pieces for each large star, for a total of three stars. Follow the diagram to lay out each one, following the A, B, C key to make stars within stars **(FIGURE 17)**; for each star, alternate which colors are A, B, and C (so a different color will be in the outer ring for each star). Lay out all three stars before you start to sew, then hand-sew the stars together in sections of nine diamonds, as shown, to make 6 diamond sections. Sew the sections together to form a star.

12 You will need six pieces for each small yellow star. Make two **(FIGURE 18)**.

13 Press all the stars so the edges are nice and crisp, clip the basting stitches, and then carefully remove the papers.

14 Center the large stars on top of the large pieced pocket blocks, and the small stars on the small pieced pockets. Match up the center vertical seam line of each star with the center seam line on each pocket. Pin each star in place, then machine-stitch or hand appliqué the stars.

15 To quilt the pockets, center each large pocket on a large batting piece, and center the small pockets on a small batting strip. Quilt as desired. The example was quilted with a swirl design on the background, and the star was not quilted. Trim the pockets back to size.

16 Line the large pockets and fuse a piece of heavy-weight interfacing to the back of each of the large pocket pieces. Pin the 14½ x 15½-inch (36.8 x 39.4 cm) background pieces on top of each pocket, right sides facing. Stitch them together along the long (horizontal) edges. Turn right sides out.

note: *The background pieces are bigger than the pocket pieces but once the pieces are turned right side out the background piece will be both a lining to the pocket and the binding.*

17 Repeat step 16 for the small pockets, using the remaining interfacing and the background fabric pieces.

18 Attach the pockets:
- ☐ Lay the completed pockets onto the background piece **(FIGURE 19)** and pin in place.
- ☐ Stitch ½-inch (1.3 cm) from the edge, down both sides of the organizer. Stitch a seam along the bottom of each pocket.
- ☐ To divide the small pockets into sections, stitch an additional seam down the two outer seams through all layers, backstitching a couple of times at the top for strength. This will give you one larger pocket in the center and one small pocket on each side.

19 To make the hanging loops, cut two pieces of cotton twill tape 3 inches (7.6 cm) long. Fold these in half and place them on the wrong side of the hanging organizer, at each corner. Pin them ½ inch (1.3 cm) in from the sides and stitch them ⅛ inch (3 mm) away from the top edge. Backstitch a few times to make sure that they are stitched on securely.

20 To finish up, bind the edges of the organizer pages 136-137. Attach two hooks to the wall or the back of the door, and hang it up!

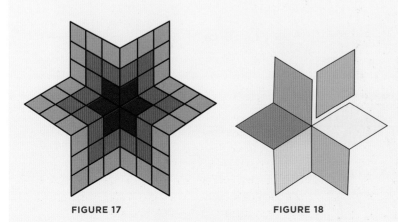

FIGURE 17

FIGURE 18

FIGURE 19

◆ dream garden diamonds quilt

by John Q. Adams ■ finished size: 56 x 72 inches (142.2 x182.9 cm) ■ quilted by Angela Walters

The design of this quilt was inspired by its whimsical fabrics, which are highlighted in the diamond blocks. Simple squares are set on point to create a field of diamonds across the quilt top. The alternating blocks and use of negative space create a secondary diamond pattern reminiscent of a garden lattice.

materials

- ☐ 1 yard (.9 m) of a main focus fabric (you'll need more if fussy cutting images)
- ☐ 7 different ¼-yard (.2 m) cuts of assorted coordinating fabrics
- ☐ 3⅔ yards (3.4 m) of white solid fabric
- ☐ 4½ yards (4.1 m) of backing fabric
- ☐ 1 piece of batting, 64 x 80 inches (162.6 x 203.2 cm)
- ☐ ⅔ yard (.7 m) of binding fabric

cutting

1 From the main focus fabric, cut 17 squares measuring 8½ inches (21.6 cm). If fussy cutting, be sure your cut image is as close to the center of your cut square as possible.

2 From assorted coordinating fabrics, cut a total of:
- ☐ 18 rectangles measuring 4½ x 8½ inches (11.4 x 21.6 cm)
- ☐ 24 squares measuring 4½ inches (11.4 cm)
- ☐ 124 rectangles measuring 2½ x 6½ inches (6.4 x 16.5 cm)

3 From the white solid fabric, cut:
- ☐ 128 squares measuring 4½ inches (11.4 cm)
- ☐ 125 squares measuring 4½ inches (11.4 cm), then cut them in half diagonally to make triangles

- -

assembly

1 The quilt is comprised of 63 blocks: 32 A blocks and 31 B blocks. There are three variations of A blocks. The instructions will detail how to construct all four block types (A-1, A-2, A-3, and B). Start by drawing a diagonal line on the back of the 128 white squares.

2 How to make block A-1:
- ☐ Position one of the marked white squares in the upper left corner of a focus fabric square. Stitch a seam along the drawn line **(FIGURE 20)**. Trim the excess fabric from the corner ¼-inch (.6 cm) from the seam.
- ☐ In the same way, stitch white squares to the remaining three corners of the block. Press seams open **(FIGURE 21)**.
- ☐ Repeat this process with the remaining 16 focus fabric squares, to make a total of 17 A-1 blocks measuring 8½ inches (21.6 cm) square.

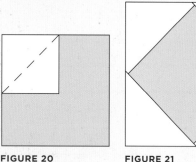

FIGURE 20   **FIGURE 21**

3 How to make block A-2:
- ☐ Join two of the 4½ x 8½-inch (11.4 x 21.6 cm) print rectangles together along the 8½-inch (21.6 cm) edge.
- ☐ Position one of the marked white squares in the upper left corner, as you did in step 2 **(FIGURE 22)**. Stitch along the drawn line and trim the excess fabric.
- ☐ Stitch a marked white square to all four corners.
- ☐ Use the remaining print rectangles of the same size to make a total of nine A-2 blocks **(FIGURE 23)**.

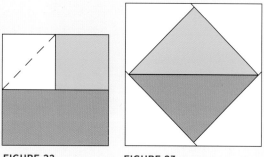

FIGURE 22   **FIGURE 23**

4 How to make block A-3:
- ☐ Join two 4½-inch (11.4 cm) print squares together. Repeat with another two print squares, then join the two rows to create a four-patch unit measuring 8½ inches (21.6 cm) square **(FIGURE 24)**.
- ☐ Join marked white squares to all four corners, as done with the previous A blocks **(FIGURE 25)**. Press seams open.
- ☐ Use the remaining print squares to make a total of six A-3 blocks.

note: *You may also choose to make block A-3 using a half-square triangle method (page 131), if you prefer.*

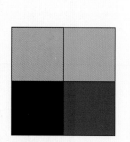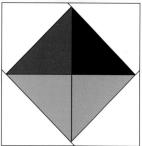

FIGURE 24   **FIGURE 25**

5 How to make block B:

☐ Use the remaining print strips and remaining white triangles to make these blocks.

☐ For each quadrant of the block, lay a rectangle between the two triangles and stitch them together **(FIGURE 26)**. Press seams toward the middle unit, and trim to 4½ inches (11.4 cm) square.

☐ Make three more quadrants.

☐ Position the quadrants so the diagonal strips form a cross **(FIGURE 27)**. Stitch the rows together to make a block. Trim the block to 8½ inches (21.6 cm) square.

☐ Repeat this process to make 31 B-blocks.

6 To assemble the quilt top:

☐ Lay out the quilt blocks out in a 7 x 9 block grid, alternating the A and B blocks. Mix in the A-1, A-2, and A-3 blocks as you like, for an eye-pleasing layout.

☐ Stitch the blocks together in rows, and then join rows together.

7 Refer to page 135-137 for tips on basting, quilting, and binding your quilt.

FIGURE 26

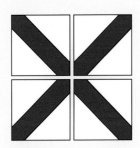

FIGURE 27

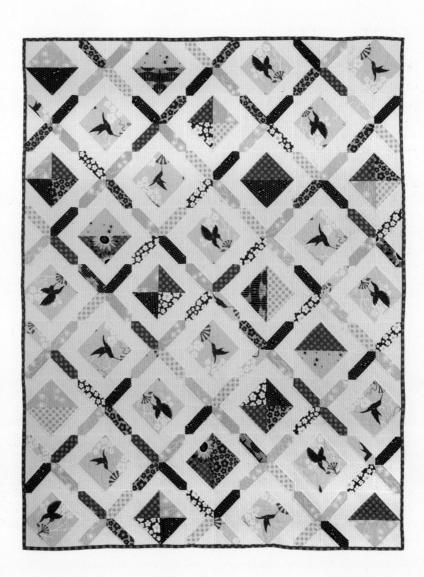

quilting basics

Whether you've made one quilt or 100, a little refresher is always nice. Here are a few terms, tips, and techniques to orient you to the blocks and projects in this book.

block sizes

All of the blocks in this book are 12 inches (30.5 cm) finished (when sewn into a quilt). While blocks can be any size, a 12-inch (30.5 cm) finished block is the standard size used in quilting bees, and it's the perfect size for new quilters. The size of the individual pieces makes them easier to construct (no piece is too tiny), and you don't need to make too many blocks to end up with a nice-sized lap quilt.

seam allowance

All of the projects in this book use a ¼-inch (6 mm) seam allowance unless otherwise stated.

Mastering the ¼-inch (6 mm) seam is key to achieving better points and perfection in your patchwork! Most modern sewing machines come with a patchwork or ¼-inch (6 mm) seam foot as standard, but if not, check your machine's manual, and ask at your local sewing shop or wherever you shop online.

Test your ¼-inch (6 mm) seam by lining the right hand edge of the foot with the edge of the fabric you are sewing and sew in a straight line. Measure it with a ruler **(FIGURE 1)**.

note: *Machines tend to be just over or under a precise ¼ inch (6 mm) so account for that by sewing either slightly more or less generously to the edge.*

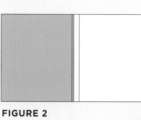

FIGURE 2

FIGURE 3

pressing

Once you have sewn your seams, the next step in neat and tidy patchwork is setting them with an iron.

First, make sure you press on the stitched line; don't iron by moving your iron around as this will distort the fabric. Simply press down gently, lift, press down again, and repeat until you have set the entire seam.

Traditionally seams were pressed to one side to reinforce the seam. With modern sewing machines, this is not necessary as a machine-stitched seam is already very strong. However, many people prefer the ease of pressing to one side. Always press towards the darker fabric so that the seam allowance doesn't show through to the patchwork **(FIGURE 2)**.

Pressing seams open makes the patchwork lay flatter and reduces bulk in the seams **(FIGURE 3)**. This is particularly useful if you're piecing something with many points that meet and form a bulky lump, as in the Eight-Pointed star block on page 73, or if appliquéing over the seams, as in Orange Soda Redux, see page 33.

Take the time to try both methods to find which you prefer.

FIGURE 1

basic quilting units

Here are the basic building blocks of many quilts and quilt blocks.

Half-Square Triangles

Half-square triangles are used in many of the blocks and projects in this book, particularly in the triangle chapter (page 50). Here's a quick trick for making multiple half square triangles.

1 First, decide the size you'd like your half-square triangle to be. Cut two squares that are ½ inch (1.3 cm) taller and wider than the unfinished size of your desired half-square triangle. For example, if the half-square triangle measures 2 inches (5 cm) in the finished block, it will need to be 2½ inches (6.4 cm) unfinished and therefore you'll need to start with two 3-inch (7.6 cm) squares.

2 Place two squares together with right sides facing. Draw a line down the diagonal on the wrong side of one of the squares **(FIGURE 4)**.

3 Sew ¼ inch (6 mm) from the drawn line on both sides **(FIGURE 5)**.

4 Cut along the drawn line. Press and trim to the desired size. You will now have two half-square triangles **(FIGURE 6)**.

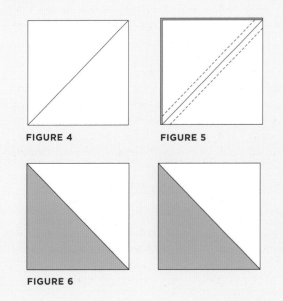

FIGURE 4   FIGURE 5

FIGURE 6

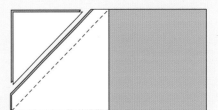

FIGURE 7

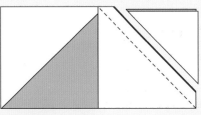

FIGURE 8

Flying Geese

Flying geese are another traditional quilt element with lots of design potential, and we've used them in numerous ways throughout the book. Here are the basics steps for creating flying geese units.

1 Decide the size you'd like your finished flying geese unit to be. Cut two squares that are ½ inch (1.3 cm) taller than your desired geese unit and one rectangle that is ½ inch (1.3 cm) taller and wider than your desired geese unit. For example, if you'd like to create a 2 x 4-inch (5 x 10.2 cm) flying geese unit, cut two 2½-inch (6.4 cm) squares and one rectangle that measures 2½ x 4½ inches (6.4 x 11.4 cm).

2 Draw a line along the diagonal on the back of each square. Line one square up with the edge of the rectangle. Sew along the diagonal line, and trim ¼ inch (6 mm) from the seam line **(FIGURE 7)**.

3 Line up the other square on the other side of the rectangle so that it overlaps the edge of the first square. Sew along the diagonal line, and trim ¼ inch (6 mm) from the seam **(FIGURE 8)**. Open and press.

other techniques

Many of the blocks and quilts in this book involve some extra techniques for quilt top construction or added embellishment.

Appliqué

Appliqué simply means fixing smaller pieces of fabric to a larger foundation to form shapes or pictures. There are many ways to achieve this, but the fastest and easiest way is by machine.

free-motion machine appliqué

In Orange Soda Quilt (page 46), the appliquéd petal shapes are free-motion stitched onto the quilt top. For this you will need a free motion, appliqué, or darning foot (essentially the same foot you would use for free-motion quilting).

Following the manufacturers guidelines, fuse your shapes to the quilt top using fusible web.

1 Use a new sharp needle, lower or cover the feed dogs on your machine and attach your darning, free motion, or appliqué foot. Set your stitch length to zero.

2 Start off by manually bringing the needle down and up again and pull the bobbin thread up to the top of the quilt top. Make a few stitches in the same place to form a kind of knot and secure the stitches. Then set your needle in the down position.

3 Follow the edges of the fused shapes and try to stitch just inside them, approximately ⅛ inch (3 mm) from the edge. If you miss a bit, simply turn the quilt top and go back over that part. Think of the stitches as casually sketching around the shapes.

tip: *Hold the quilt top tightly in your hands and move at a steady speed—too fast and your stitches will be too long, too slow and they will be too short.*

You can also use zigzag stitch, buttonhole stitch, or satin stitch for machine appliqué.

hand appliqué

This type of hand appliqué is perfect when you don't want the stitching to show.

First, pin the appliqué securely to your background fabric, and using thread that matches your background fabric make very small whip stitches approximately ¼ inch (6 mm) apart around the perimeter of the shapes, turning under the edges as you work. The smaller your stitches, the tidier the result.

tip: *Special appliqué pins—shorter than regular pins—can make this process easier.*

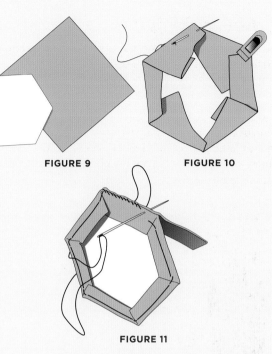

FIGURE 9

FIGURE 10

FIGURE 11

English Paper Piecing

English paper piecing is a method of hand stitching shapes together using fabric folded and basted over paper template shapes. It makes complicated shapes much easier to piece perfectly. All you need are templates, thread for basting, and thread for sewing the shapes together. You can find many graph paper sites online, create your own templates, or buy pre-cut templates from quilt stores.

To explain English paper piecing, we'll show you how to sew hexagons together.

1 Cut your fabrics into squares about ¼ inch (6 mm) or so larger than your templates, all the way round **(FIGURE 9)**. You can leave them as squares or cut them into more precise shapes.

2 Center the paper template on the wrong side of your fabric. Fold up one side, carefully feeling for the edge of the template and folding along this line. Fold the second side in the same way to form a corner.

tip: *Clip this first corner with either a regular paper clip or some other small clip to keep it from slipping as you baste all the way round.*

3 Grab a hand sewing needle and a piece of thread with a knotted end. Fold up the second corner of the shape, just like the first corner, but instead of fixing with a clip, sew a couple of stitches through the fabric to hold in place. Continue around the shape, sewing the fabric but taking care not to sew through the paper template **(FIGURE 10)**. Don't pull the stitches too tight or you might distort the template.

tip: *Sewing around the template rather than through them enables you to reuse the papers, puts less pressure on your hands if you have many pieces to sew and also means you don't have to remove the tacking stitches later.*

4 Place your shapes right sides together, and use a whipstitch to sew them together **(FIGURE 11)**. Take care to sew from corner to corner of the edges to avoid holes in the finished patchwork. Finish by backstitching each edge for added strength.

5 Once the patchwork is complete, remove all the paper templates working from the center out.

FUSSY CUTTING

Fussy cutting is when specific motifs or design features are cut to fit the shapes required for patchwork. Perhaps you want to frame a novelty print, or even try and create a kaleidoscope effect; both are done using fussy cutting. And here's how:

If you're cutting a straightforward shape such as a square, the easiest way to fussy cut is by using a transparent ruler. Simply center your motif in the square, and cut it out.

If you're using more complicated shapes, it is easier to use transparent plastic templates. Trace around your paper template onto transparent template plastic, and cut out the shape. Use the template on the right side of the fabric to find the best fit for the design element you wish to fussy cut. Trace around the template and cut out your fabric piece.

Foundation Piecing

Foundation piecing is when block pieces are sewn together onto a template drawn on either a paper or a fabric base. The patterns in this book use paper foundations as a temporary guide for making blocks.

1 To make the template, simply draw or copy the mirror image of the block onto the paper of your choice **(FIGURE 12)**. Do not add any seam allowances.

note: *Since the block is sewn together along the drawn lines on the paper with the fabric on the other side of the paper, the sewn block will be the mirror image of the drawn block.*

2 Cut a piece of fabric larger than the first piece on your template and arrange it on the backside of the template so that it overhangs by at least ¼ inch (6 mm) on all sides **(FIGURE 13)**. You can use a dab of glue or pin to hold the piece in place.

3 Cut a piece of fabric larger than the second piece on your template, and line it up with the first fabric piece so that they overlap the line dividing the two pieces by at least ¼ inch (6 mm) **(FIGURE 14)**.

4 Turn the paper template over and sew along the line dividing piece 1 and piece 2. Use a short stitch length so the close perforations make the paper easier to remove.

5 Open up the second fabric piece and check that it covers the second patch on your template by at least ¼ inch (6 mm) on all sides. Trim the seam allowance to ¼ inch (6 mm), open, and press **(FIGURE 15)**.

6 Repeat for the remaining pieces in your template, making sure all the outside edges of the block extend ¼ inch (6 mm) beyond the template **(FIGURE 16)**.

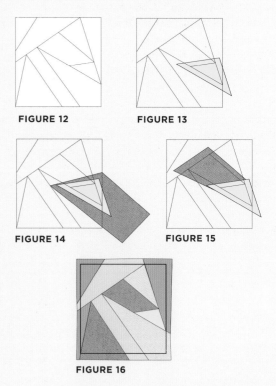

FIGURE 12

FIGURE 13

FIGURE 14

FIGURE 15

FIGURE 16

assembly

Putting a quilt together involves the same basic steps but is never quite the same process twice.

Stacking and Basting

A quilt sandwich consists of three layers: the patchwork quilt top, the batting and the backing. To avoid wrinkles and puckers in your quilting, you need to make a good sandwich. Use a large, clean floor area and ensure your quilt top and backing are both well pressed and all the seams lie flat. Trim off any stray threads.

1 First, make sure your backing should be at least 2 inches (5 cm) larger than your quilt top all the way round. Make your backing a little larger than your batting so you can see all three layers as you baste.

2 Lay your backing right side down on the floor, smooth out the wrinkles and secure the edges with painters tape (or masking tape) at regular intervals. Pull the backing gently to make it smooth but don't pull it too taut or stretch the fabric. Start at the top edge of the backing, then the bottom edge and finally both sides.

3 Lay your batting on the backing, making sure it's inside the edges of the backing all the way round. Smooth out the wrinkles gently from the center out to the edges.

4 Center the quilt top, right side up, on top of the batting. Gently smooth out the wrinkles from the center out.

5 Pin all three layers together using special quilters' safety pins, which have a handy curved edge. Start at the center and pin towards the edges in a grid pattern. Pin approximately every 5 inches (12.7 cm) or use your hand width as a rough guide. The more pins, the better basted your quilt will be and the likelihood of wrinkles is reduced.

6 Put an extra pin in each corner to secure the layers.

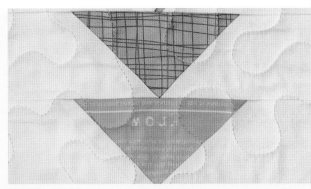

FIGURE 17

Quilting

Quilting's most basic purpose is to keep your three layers together and to prevent them from shifting, but quilting itself can become part of the overall quilt design and good quilting will enhance your patchwork.

The projects in this book were all machine quilted. The larger projects were professionally quilted by long-arm machine quilters. To find a good long-arm quilter, start at your local quilt shop or local quilt guild. Prices vary depending on what kind of design you choose. A loose and simple allover pattern (called a pantograph) is usually the cheapest design **(FIGURE 17)**. After that, the more closely (or densely) quilted the design, the more expensive it becomes **(FIGURE 18)**. The most expensive type of professional quilting is custom quilting, where the quilter free-motion quilts different designs in different areas of the quilt to bring out the absolute best in the design **(FIGURE 19)**.

If you don't have a local guild or shop, then ask other quilters you know for their recommendations or use the computer to search online. Before committing to anything, have a few conversations with the quilter, get a clear price guide, and look at examples of their work. Many local quilt shops even have a machine to hire and offer some basic teaching. If you would prefer to try and quilt yourself, and that option is available to you, consider it. The quilting process is much neater when the three layers are rolled onto a large frame, and you have a larger surface area to work with.

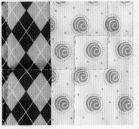

FIGURE 18

FIGURE 19

quilting basics

straight-line quilting

If you do decide to do the quilting yourself using a domestic machine, there are many options available to you, starting with simple straight-line quilting.

Start by marking a quilting design on your patchwork quilt top. You should do this before basting. Use a water-soluble or fading pen, a pencil that is specific for marking quilts, or tailor's chalk. Test the pen or pencil first before marking your finished top. Special quilter's gloves, or even gardening gloves with grips on the fingers and palms, are invaluable for machine quilting. They help you to keep a tight control on the quilt as you move it around.

To quilt straight lines, you'll need a walking foot for your machine. This foot keeps your three layers from bunching or wrinkling as you work. Choose a spot to begin your quilting; a centerline down or across the middle of the quilt is the best place to start.

Bring your bobbin thread up to the surface of the quilt, and stitch a few stitches in one place or use very small stitches (reduce the stitch length to almost zero) to fix the quilting and prevent your stitches from coming undone later. Return your stitch length to the normal length, and quilt your first line to the edge of the quilt, stopping just before the edge and reducing the stitch length again to fix the stitches in place. Turn the quilt 90° and do the same again. Repeat for all the straight lines in the quilt. To prevent the quilt from bunching up and getting in the way as you work, you can roll it up under the machine arm and unroll/roll up as necessary.

When you have stabilized the quilt with straight lines, you can then free-motion quilt particular areas to enhance your design, without having to negotiate quilting pins every few inches. Or, if you prefer, create more straight lines. You can also go across in the opposite direction to create a cross-hatch effect.

free-motion quilting

If you intend to free-motion quilt (like drawing with your stitches), you'll need a free-motion foot or darning foot. You also need to make sure the feed dogs (which are the little jagged teeth underneath the sewing machine foot that help guide the fabric through the machine smoothly) can be covered or dropped (refer to the manual that came with your machine).

Practice with a pencil and piece of paper a few times to get a feel for it before you start.

Choose a central point in the block or area you want to quilt, and fix the stitches as before. If you have marked a design on the quilt, follow the lines holding the quilt firmly and moving at a steady speed. Free-motion quilting takes practice and your first efforts might not be perfect. Having a few practice runs using smaller projects such as the placemats **(FIGURE 20)** or a pillow is a good idea.

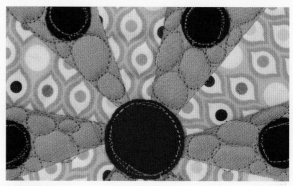

FIGURE 20

Binding

Binding your quilt is the final step in finishing your quilt. It hides the raw edges of the quilt top, batting and backing and frames your finished piece. You may choose a fabric that matches the background fabric, or use scraps left over from your blocks, or even audition fabrics specifically to add interest to the finished look. Think carefully as to what fabric to use, try laying out your quilt top next to different possible choices. You don't want the binding to distract from the patchwork.

We used two main forms of binding in this book: straight-edge binding (which uses straight-cut fabric strips on the grain of the fabric which makes the binding less likely to stretch as you attach it to the quilt) and bias binding (which uses strips cut on the bias, across the grain of the fabric which makes the binding stretch a little). For the projects in this book, you only really need straight edge binding which uses less fabric and is quicker and easier to do. But if you are binding a curved project, we recommend you use bias binding.

tip: *Binding clips can be found at many quilt stores or online. If you can't find them, you can use hairclips instead. You may also want to use a thimble to protect your fingertips.*

straight-edge binding

Here are the basic steps for straight-edge binding.

1 Measure the perimeter of your quilt and add 10 inches (25.4 cm). This is the length of binding you will need.

2 Cut enough strips 2½ inches (5 cm) x width of fabric (selvedge to selvedge) to make up your required length.

3 Sew the strips together end to end (with a ¼-inch [6 mm] seam allowance) to make one long strip.

4 Fold the strip in half widthwise, with wrong sides together, and press to make a strip 1¼ inches (3.2 cm) x the required length

5 Trim the excess backing and batting so they're the same size as the quilt top.

6 Pin the raw edge of the binding to the edge of the front (patchwork side) of the quilt in the center of one edge, leaving a tail of about 5 inches (12.7 cm). Pin up to the first corner, and sew the binding in place using a ¼-inch (6 mm) seam. Stop ¼ inch (6 mm) away from the first corner and backstitch to secure.

7 Fold the binding strip up at a 90° angle **(FIGURE 21)**. Fold back down toward the quilt and parallel to the next edge. Pin in place.

8 Sew the mitered corner from the very edge, on top of the fold and onwards **(FIGURE 22)**. Continue on until you reach your next corner, and repeat

9 Sew until you get to a point 4 inches (10.2 cm) away from where you started the binding. Backstitch a couple of times. Leave another 5 inches (12.7 cm) of binding free and discard any leftovers. Bring both ends of the binding together fold back on to themselves, so that the newly folded edges meet right sides together—but don't overlap—and press.

10 Now here's the slightly awkward bit. You'll need to sew along the folds to join your binding ends together. First, fold your quilt back and the binding outwards and pin either side of the fold. Sew along the fold, backstitching at either end **(FIGURE 23)**. Trim the excess, and press the seam open to reduce bulk. Sew the last few inches of your binding to the quilt as before, and you're done!

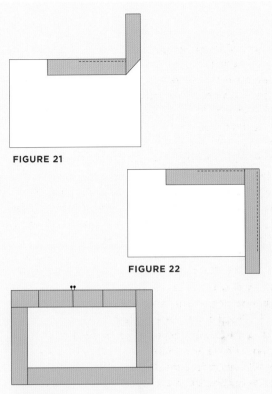

FIGURE 21

FIGURE 22

FIGURE 23

hand stitching the binding

You'll next need to hand stitch the binding in place on the back of the quilt. For this part of the process, gather binding clips, a sharp hand-sewing needle, and thread to match your binding.

1 Start in the center of one edge and fold the binding over toward the back of your quilt. Use binding clips to secure a section of binding in place. Use about one clip every 5 inches (12.7 cm) or so.

2 Cut a length of thread approximately hand to elbow length and tie a knot at one end. Hand stitch the binding to the back of the quilt by sewing through the backing and batting and taking the needle back through the very edge of the binding. Take care not to sew all the way through to the front of your quilt. Make a whip stitch every ¼ inch (6 mm) or so and continue to the first corner.

3 When you reach the first corner sew right up to the very edge of the quilt and then fold the mitered corner back down and continue sewing the next edge.

4 Continue on around the whole quilt.

templates

*Seam allowance is included
for all templates requiring it

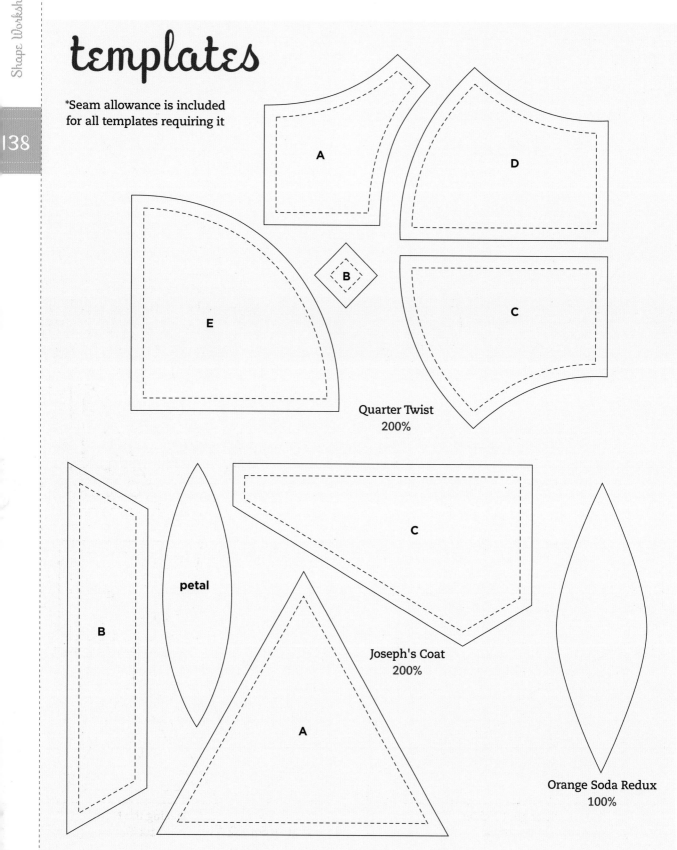

A

D

B

E

C

Quarter Twist
200%

petal

C

B

A

Joseph's Coat
200%

Orange Soda Redux
100%

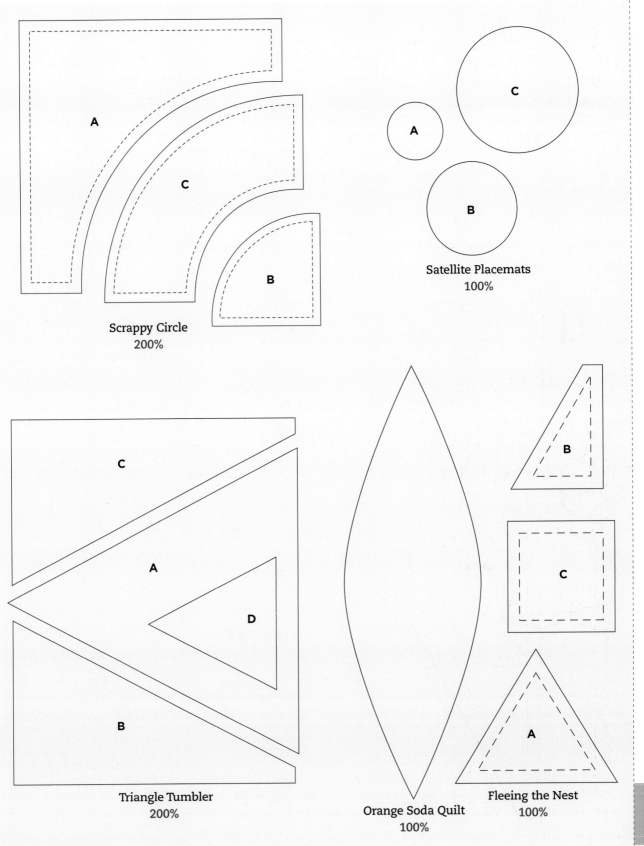

A

C

B

Scrappy Circle
200%

C

A

B

Satellite Placemats
100%

C

A

D

B

Triangle Tumbler
200%

B

C

A

Orange Soda Quilt
100%

Fleeing the Nest
100%

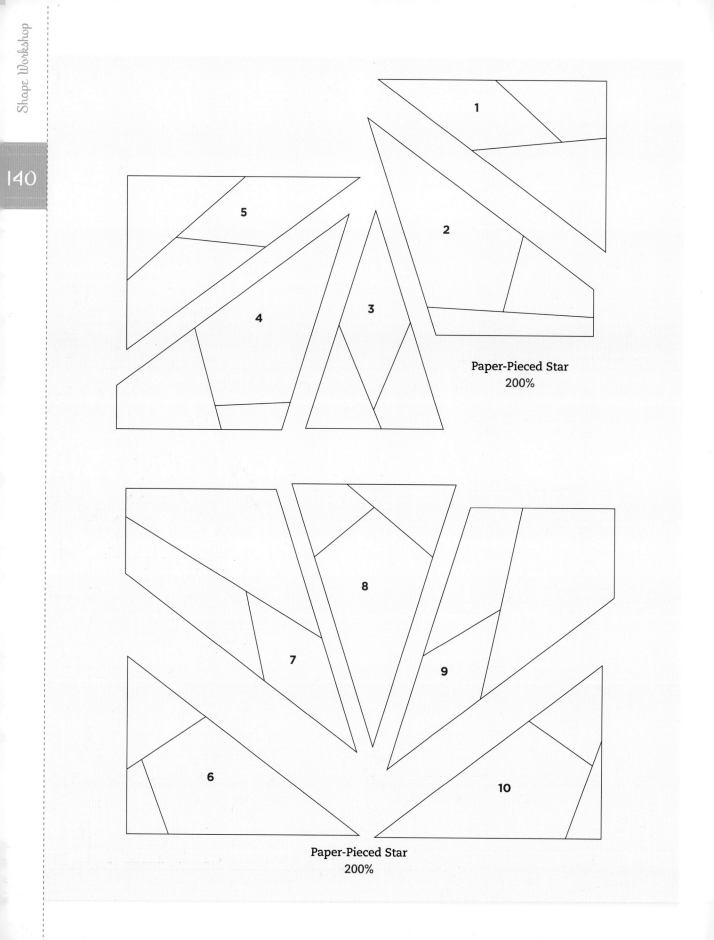

Paper-Pieced Star
200%

Paper-Pieced Star
200%

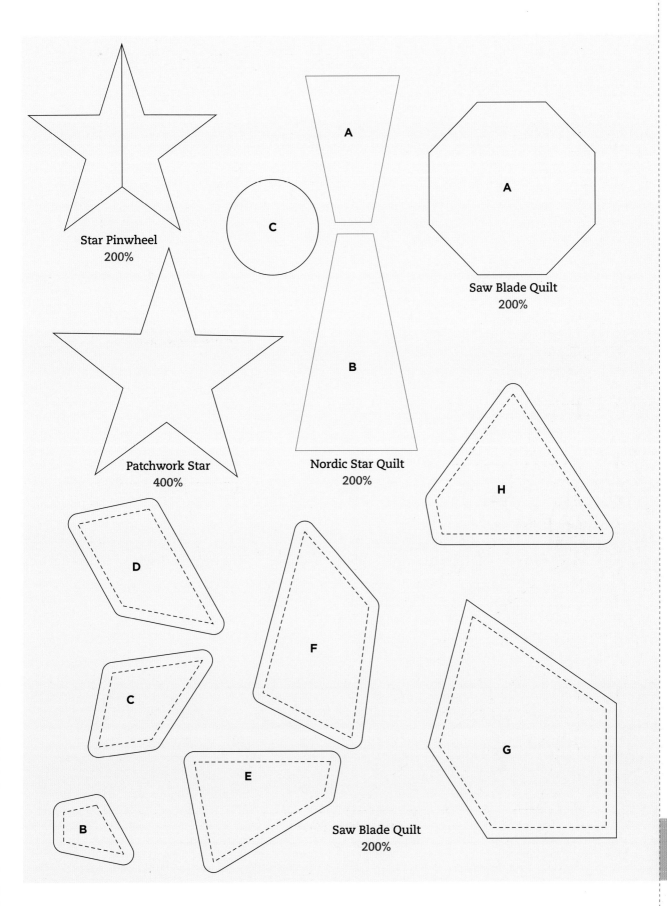

Star Pinwheel
200%

A

C

A

Saw Blade Quilt
200%

Patchwork Star
400%

B

Nordic Star Quilt
200%

H

D

F

G

C

E

B

Saw Blade Quilt
200%

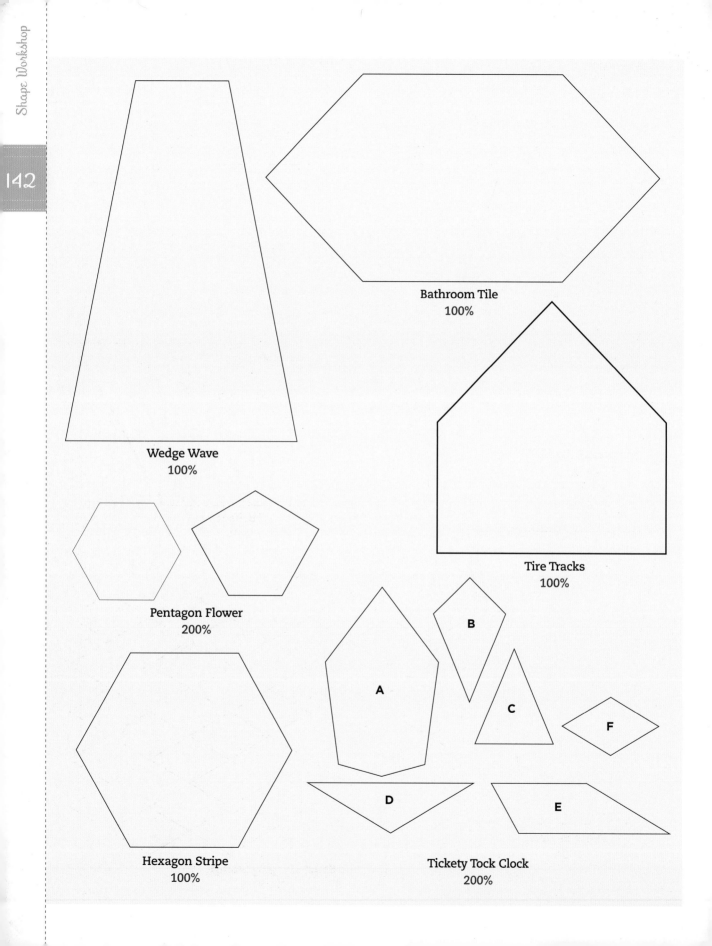

Wedge Wave
100%

Bathroom Tile
100%

Tire Tracks
100%

Pentagon Flower
200%

A

B

C

D

E

F

Hexagon Stripe
100%

Tickety Tock Clock
200%

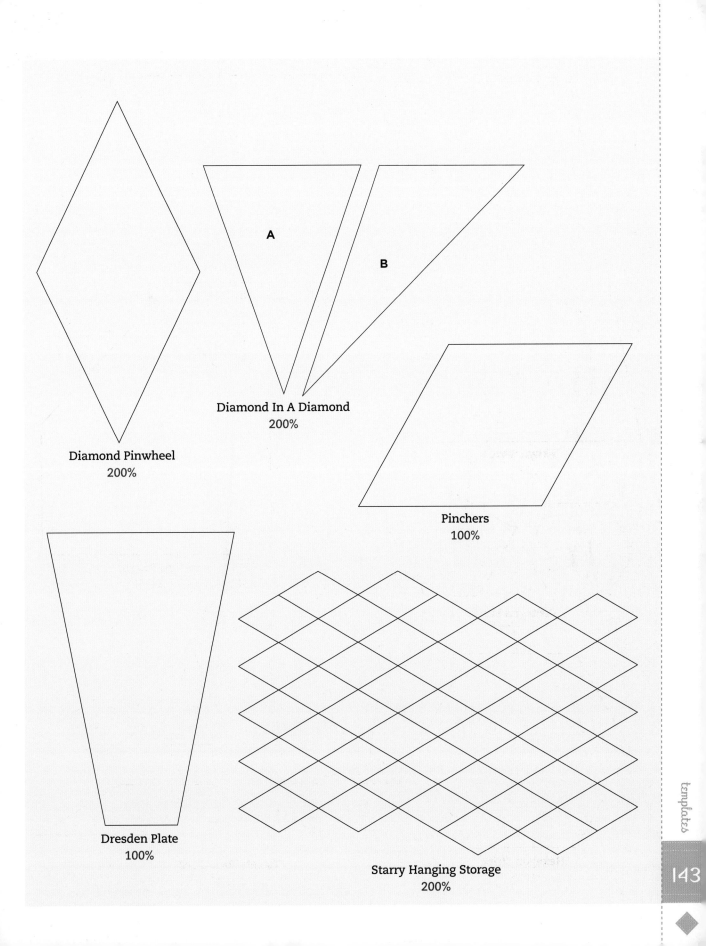

Diamond Pinwheel
200%

A

B

Diamond In A Diamond
200%

Pinchers
100%

Dresden Plate
100%

Starry Hanging Storage
200%

acknowledgments

We couldn't have written this book without the support and encouragement of so many people. A huge thank you to our ever-growing community and Fat Quarterly readers. The faith and continued support you have in us pushes us to work harder with each new issue. You are our rock, and without you we would still be four friends across the globe chatting to each other about our shared love of quilting—now we can chat with you as well!

Massive thanks and so much love to our original founder members, Aneela Hoey, Kate Dixon, and Nova Flitter who helped us get to this point. We couldn't have done it without you.

To Amanda at Lark Crafts for being there from the start and nudging us along in the journey of this book—thank you.

Thank you to the fabric companies and designers that showed support and provided fabrics for the projects in the *Fat Quarterly Shape Workshop.*

And the biggest thank you to our own families—to Luis, Kiely, Warren, and Sandy—and our children who some-times get fed takeaway for three nights running or only one (short) story at bedtime. You live amongst our growing stacks of fabric and quilts, you put up with stray threads on your clothes. You rarely complain. We love you!

The following fabric companies and designers were used for the projects in the *Fat Quarterly Shape Workshop:*

MODA FABRICS (WWW.UNITEDNOTIONS.COM)

ROBERT KAUFMAN FABRICS (WWW.ROBERTKAUFMAN.COM)

MICHAEL MILLER FABRICS (WWW.MICHAELMILLERFABRICS.COM)

JENNIFER MOORE, MONALUNA (WWW.MONALUNA.COM)

MICHELLE BENCSKO, CLOUD NINE (WWW.CLOUD9FABRICS.COM)

SAFFRON CRAIG (WWW.SAFFRONCRAIG.COM)

KOKKA/ECHINO (WWW.SEVENISLANDSFABRIC.COM)

index